The purpose of this book is to educate and entertain. The author and publishers of this book do not dispense medical or psychological advice. You should not use the techniques herein for treatment of any physical or medication issues without seeking the advice of a qualified medical practitioner. In the event you use any advice from this book, the author and publisher assume no responsibility for your actions.

Matthew Wadsworth

# EVEN THE DAYLIGHT APPEARED DARK

"A Journey through Life, the Military, Depression
and Post Traumatic Stress Disorder"

authorHOUSE®

*AuthorHouse*™
*1663 Liberty Drive*
*Bloomington, IN 47403*
*www.authorhouse.com*
*Phone: 1-800-839-8640*

*First published by AuthorHouse 02/21/2011*

*ISBN: 978-1-4567-7504-9 (sc)*
*ISBN: 978-1-4567-7534-6 (e)*

*Printed in the United States of America*

This book is dedicated to old friends and new, thanks for sharing some of my journey, I cannot express in words what you have helped me to achieve.

To all those who have served or are still serving, families and friends of the Armed Forces, I am very proud and honoured to have once served alongside you, I wish you all the happiness life can bring.

*Matt Wadsworth*

# CONTENTS

To protect the identity of people mentioned in this book, nobody has a name.

Acknowledgements:

This book would not have seen daylight and would have remained in the dark if it wasn't for the help of some very special people.

I would like to thank all my family and friends. I am lucky to have friends that I class as family, maybe not by blood but by a deeper bond. I know our journeys have had their bumps, twists and turns, thank you for the unconditional love and support you have shown me. All journeys go in different directions, if ours are no longer on the same bearing, I wish you and your families are safe and happy. I look forward to the day when our paths cross again.

Thanks to all those at Talking2Minds for believing and supporting me, I am very proud to be apart of the team and have you as friends.

My eternal thanks go to Tom Evans, aka The Bookwright, for taking my first draft and editing into what you read here. Tom's deft touch with words is literally enlightening. If you have an idea for a book or a book in formation, Tom is the person to contact to make it a reality.

I'd also like to thank Fay Miller the books proof reader who has such an attention to detail.

Thanks to AuthorHouse Publishing for seeing the value in my story and for adding it to there portfolio of amazing titles.

Collectively, the skills and professionalism of these people are what have made the difference between this being an MS Word file gathering virtual dust on my hard drive and the book you hold in your hands.

*The title of this book says it all!*
*I know as I've been there.*
*Only someone who has experienced the isolation, panic and sheer bloody anguish of Post Traumatic Stress Disorder (PTSD) can fully understand its implications.*

*As Matthew states quite eloquently, this illness is perceived as a cop out, make believe and a pitiful excuse, when in reality it destroys the life of not only the sufferer but the lives of those forced to watch their tortured descent into their own personal hell.*

*Matthew's book, I hope, will succeed in enlightening the uninitiated and offer a glimmer of hope to those going through the trauma and nightmare of PTSD.*

*The book takes you on a painful journey that will help to throw a ray of light into the perpetual darkness of this infernal illness.*

*Matthew shows us that a way out is possible, and that traditional therapies are not the only way. There are alternative treatments that can make a difference.*

*He shows us by lighting a matchstick of possibilities, that with the right help it can become a flame to light us out of the darkness.*

**Simon Weston OBE**

In 1982 the Sir Galahad was destroyed in Bluff Cove on the Falkland Islands. On board was Simon Weston, a Welsh Guardsman. A name and a face that would become well known for his struggle to overcome his injuries (46% burns) and would redefine his role in life. Following his injuries, Simon's road to physical, spiritual and mental recovery saw him active in a number of highly successful ventures.

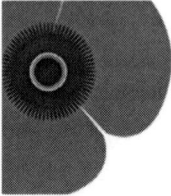

*PTSD is a disability which is invisible to many of us and is not always properly understood. The symptoms can be difficult to manage and many employers are fearful of employing people with Mental Health conditions.*

*We at the Royal British Legion Poppy Factory are extremely proud to support Matthew and many other ex-Servicemen and women like him, with a range of difficulties and disabilities, into the world of paid civilian employment. Our Clients work in a variety of charitable and commercial organizations in many locations across the UK. Our Employment Scheme offers clients a step onto the employment ladder with employers who are prepared to overcome disability barriers.*

*Matthew has chosen to work for an organization called Quantum Performance and he also volunteers for the charity Talking2Minds, which helped and supported him and now he helps others.*

*Sometimes those who have experienced disabilities personally are often best placed to help support others with the same condition. There are several organisations committed to helping those with PTSD and many of those who run them have had similar experiences. We all aim to provide these men and women with the very best support we can and we find that employment is often one of the steps towards recovery.*

This is a very honest book. Most people have only peeped through cracks in the front door, but Matthew invites us in to the house and lets us explore most of the rooms. His experiences are extraordinary and he displays enormous courage in exposing his feelings and sufferings to us. Matthew is delivering a tremendous service to all who suffer from this condition by this exposure.

We all owe an enormous debt to all of our ex-Service men and women, including Matthew.

***Melanie Waters LLB MBA***
***Chief Executive,***
***The Royal British Legion Poppy Factory***

This book is my life, how it was, how it is and hopefully how it may continue.

Everyone has a story, mine isn't the hardest or the most difficult you will read about but it is what happened, to me, over the last 25 years.

Everything is relevant to an individual. We all have a breaking point. It may take six months, it may take 16 years; everyone remembers, no one forgets.

At some point we all break, it's just a case of when and how we fix ourselves.

For 25 years, I bottled things inside until one day the bottle burst. This is a journey through my life and hopefully at the end people will understand me and what led me to the point of suicide.

I will not hold back, a spade is a spade. I won't flower things up just to make it a good read. I will be open honest and true, and let you into a place no one has ever been, my head.

Trying to explain what the darkness is has had me thinking for days. Everyone's darkness is different. With me, it is a tiredness, not wanting to get out of bed on a morning, not having any more fight left within, and not wanting to talk to anyone or be around people. It is needing to feel pain to feel alive. It is wanting to disappear and leave everything behind; your identity, your life, but ultimately it is feeling that all your objectives are complete and there is nothing left to live for.

When I am consumed by these feelings, I have an inner

struggle, there is a good side and a bad side to me, one side is reasonable, logical and objective, the other just wants pain or in the worst times death.

Through my life I have had one fight after another; it's like being in a boxing ring. I was the fighter who kept getting knocked down, but kept getting back up to take more punishment.

I didn't know when to throw the towel in, sometimes I was knocked down and the count was between nine and ten but I still dragged myself back up.

I am lucky, I am alive.

I started writing this book before I became ill again and was diagnosed with Post Traumatic Stress Disorder (PTSD).

I had been off work yet again but this time I couldn't understand why. It had cost me loss and pain, but here is the real stinker, no one understands PTSD until it happens to them. You have to be either suffering with it or watching someone close suffer with it to recognise what it even is.

The pain my friends and colleagues suffer is all the same. The point is that even with PTSD I am not in a wheelchair. I have both arms, both legs, both eyes. Some people may think that I am a liar, weak and a coward for breaking mentally, that is your choice; that I am a coward.

Am I actually the strong one for recognising things were wrong in my head and putting up my hands and asking for help?

Ironically, one of the things you lose with having PTSD is the luxury of choice. I've had past problems and yes maybe I shouldn't have done what I did in the military, but everyone has problems some big some small. What is big or small only an individual can decide, but everyone deserves a chance.

PTSD is a label. It is a box. Putting you in a box may

be good for the doctors, but is it good for you? Trauma can happen to anyone, any time, it doesn't matter if you went to a private school or a comprehensive, or if you are an officer or another rank, we are all flesh, we are all human.

Thankfully I was saved after a friend found a charity that could help me after my second admission to a mental hospital. It was just in time, I needed help and fast, as death was a more favourable prospect. I phoned the charity called Talking2Minds and spoke with a chap called Rob. He promised they would help me and thankfully they did.

I started to write the first five chapters over a year before I went on operations in Afghanistan. I thought nothing else could trouble me. I had had treatment and I thought I was fixed. In reality, I had unloaded many things but never truly dealt with them at a level which would enable me to sleep at night. I was lucky because I was given the strength by someone to continue for a few more years, until I was ready to find my answers that would finally give me a peaceful nights rest and allow the darkness to truly leave.

What happened in Afghanistan wasn't the hardest thing I have had to deal with in life, but it's the little things what weigh you down in the end. There is no need to name any names in this book; they are people from my past, family, friends, bosses, colleagues. If a story that happened to me is similar to one of yours, why would you need names of my people, when you have your own?

I tried several treatments over the years, finally I found the right one for me. You need to find something that works for you, the one which helped me, may not help you, there is no right or wrong. I only wish some professionals could think this way too. I finally got to sort out my big things and the little ones which had burned deep inside, by the process that I was introduced too, through Talking2Minds.

I hope that by reading this it may help someone.

# Chapter One

# Overdose

"Can you hear me? Wake up, how many tablets have you taken."

I opened one eye, I was in my own bed, my head was spinning mainly due to the day's drinking session, but it may also have had something to do with the 60 500mg paracetamol tablets I had taken. I thought they were meant to cure headaches. There were three other people in the room, two paramedics and one work friend, he had called in the cavalry.

I lay there not wanting to answer, I wanted them to leave, to let me die. I was tired, I was 30 years old and for 20 years I'd had to fight through life. The question was repeated, I supposed I better answer him, "Yes I can hear you, what do you want." "Have you taken anything?"

Well, there is nothing like an obvious question. This professional, had an empty paracetamol box and there was several others next to my bed, two and two always made four.

"Yes, paracetamol." I replied. "How many?" he asked.

"About two boxes worth, around 60 I guess. Now leave and let me die."

I heard my words, it seemed strange to say them but it was the truth. He just looked at me; I turned over not wanting to take his stare and wrapped myself within my duvet.

"Just leave, I am tired, I am sick of fighting, let me die."

No answer, hopefully they will be gone soon, and then he spoke again.

"Do you want to talk about it?"

My reply wasn't pleasant, I wanted these people out, to let me sleep, I have a lifetime of sleep to catch up with and I was tired.

After what seemed like hours they were still not moving, and then he hit me with it.

"You are in the air force aren't you, what do you do?"

Bastard he had found my weakness he knew what made me tick, he knew what I would live for, he knew about my job.

"Yes and I love it, but this isn't a cry for help, I want to die. I am tired, I have fought for 20 years now I need to sleep. There is nothing left for me to do, I have achieved my goals, I have been to places around the world good and bad, I have helped make a difference, like everyone has, NOW LEAVE ME TO DIE!"

This took him aback I remember him just standing, maybe to get his sentence right, he knew I was logical, he knew I was a professional, so his next sentence had to be a good one.

"It's like this, because we are here we have to treat you, if you refuse treatment I am duty bound to call the police, they will then come and we will commit you on mental health grounds, you wouldn't want that would you? That will mess with your RAF career won't it?"

This guy was good at his job, he had found my weakness and exploited it, I couldn't handle the police as well, best I go with them, there will be a next time.

"OK, pass me some clothes my rugby shirt and tracky bottoms are next door in the wardrobe."

So I got dressed, grabbed my Valentino Rossi hat and headed for the door, one paramedic in front of me, one behind and my buddy locking the door.

The night was crisp, it was around 3am, early November. Thank god everyone will be in bed, this place is rumour central, nothing is private. If I was to live I had to pull this one out of the bag, get treated, keep my job and then I will wait until next time but next time it will just be me, no one else, no one will find me for days.

My head was awash with what to do, damage control, I had to leave the dark side of my brain and think straight I had to get work down here, tell them before anyone else did. Then I would have a chance, forget dying, I had failed, time to wake up and sort the shit I had landed myself in. I was strapped in the back of the ambulance and was plugged into the monitoring units. Then came the details, name address, date of birth etc, bloody admin you never can get away from it. The darkness seeped back in, as it always had, it caught me unaware. Let me die, just let me go. I drifted in and out, every time I drifted out I was wakened by the paramedic, this was to be a long night.

The door opened, we had rolled up to the back of the A&E department, here we go, lots of questions, lots of thinking time. I was heading into the darkness again and wished for death again. I stumbled into the department and was ushered into a private cubicle, the same one I had sat in with my wife 18 months ago when they diagnosed her with e coli. I jumped onto the bed, time for sleep and death. Outside the room I could hear the paramedic doing a handover to the nurse she would be watching over me now. I was just drifting away as she came in, with her northern accent, an accent I was used to, an accent which took me back to where I hated the most, my childhood.

Then came the questions, I had to think straight, remember I had to get out of this, I answered them all. I asked the nurse to bring in my friend from the waiting room. He was shown in, what a night he'd had, so much for booze and women.

"Mate, can you do me a favour and call the boss, ask him to come down, I need him here."

So off he went to make the call, I lay there thinking what my boss would say, he was about to be woken up at 3.30am to be told one of his guys was laid in A&E after taking an overdose. I hoped he would jump into his motor and get here soon, he could help, he could think straight and I valued his judgement, he was the best boss I had worked for, for a long time.

I began to drift again the darkness consuming every thought in my head, I was tired, I had nothing left to do in my life, I felt I had lived a lifetime at 30. I came back to, with someone calling my name, it was a voice I recognised it was my boss.

"How was I?"

"A bit fucked up. This isn't me asking for help, I am tired, I am sick of fighting, I need to end it, I need to die."

My boss looked alarmed he knew I was being serious. I didn't want to be here, so he did what he did best, logical northern thinking, this guy had been around the block, he was a fighter, he was about to fight, to help me come in from the darkness.

"The doc said they will not pump your stomach or anything, you were out too long there is nothing they can give you."

Excellent I may have done it, I may die, maybe I haven't failed.

My boss then spoke to me, "I need to understand, why you are here? Why didn't you ask for help?"

Help, that's an easy word to use, but the darkness won't let you ask, when you are in it, at first you don't realise, then things escalate. You think you have it under control, but you don't, all that happens is you spiral quicker and quicker out of control and then you snap.

"You were out yesterday drinking. Why did you beat up the mirror in the pub? Why did you try to break your hand?"

I forgot about that, I was out all day, me and a few of the lads, we had a good time and then it came, the darkness seeped into my head. I remember punching a wall and a mirror, I hated who was there staring back at me, all my bad memories were staring at me, every line on my face told a different story. My hand had swollen quite badly and I had been in the A&E department earlier that night. I was told the hand wasn't broken, but there was no reasoning with me, in my world it was. After an angry exchange of words with the doc, and a few phone calls to people, I left A&E and me and a mate headed home. I was consumed with darkness, I hated myself, when we called it a night, I got the two or three boxes of paracetamol and emptied the packets. There was a big pile of white tablets sat on my bed, I picked up handful, after handful, swallowing them all down, it was my time, my time to die.

"Boss I am sick of fighting, for 20 odd years, life has been a struggle, it has been a fight, I am tired. Look, every thing is relative to an individual, some people cope with bigger things, but over time I have been ground down, I cannot fight anymore. It's all relative, it's all relative."

I was coming back to being logical, the darkness was subsiding, I sat there and heard my words, everything is relative to an individual. I wasn't here due to a single event,

I was here due to multiple events. The nurse entered they needed blood to see what damage I had done.

"No! They aren't having any. It's my blood, go away."

I wouldn't let her take any at first; I twisted my body, refusing to let her near my arms.

"Come on mate, stop it! Let her do her job, give her some blood, what difference does it make?"

My boss was being logical again, I let her take some. Then I asked for something which I knew was the wrong thing to do, I asked to see my wife. She had left me three months ago, why did I want her, I really don't know, but I asked to see her, so they made the call.

What seemed like an age passed, people whispering, were they talking about me, did I care, not really. I was curled up, pretending to be sleeping but all the time I was planning my next escape. All I had to do was show them I was together, apologise for the inconvenience and they would let me on my way, then I could do a proper job, I could die.

She walked in, still in her work clothes, she had been working the night shift, why was she here? Who invited her? I had better be social, show her I still cared, but did I really? Or was it another attempt at being normal and not failing, I was broken.

"What's all this about?" she asked, so I went through it for what seemed like the millionth time that night, trying to explain the fight with my darkness and the loss I had incurred.

I reached for her hand, she pulled away. So she came out of duty, or was it she was due to get a shit load of money if I died, I hadn't changed my will, she was to get everything. Shit no! This isn't right, half of me wanted her back for the wrong selfish reasons, half of me didn't. She wasn't there long, soon making an excuse about someone from work had brought her here and did I need anything, but don't worry, she would be back. That went well or did it? Did I care? There was no way she was ever coming back and when I saw her leave I knew it was all over between us, there was really nothing left.

I drifted off again, the mixture of booze and tablets let me do this quite easily. I woke again. Which world was I in, the light or the dark? I didn't know, they both seemed the same. A doctor looked in and my boss left with him. Was it good or bad news? I hoped for bad, but something inside me already knew it would be good.

They both came back, "Your blood tests are back, you have loads of alcohol and paracetamol in your system."

Tell me something I didn't know; these doctors are good.

"Well, it's like this, first signs are really good, it looks like there is no damage, the only reason we can think of, is you are extremely fit, it must be all the gym hours you put in."

Typical the thing I love to do, the thing which I use to push and give me pain is the thing that saved me.

"We are going to keep you here for a few hours. When your alcohol level has subsided we will get you to talk to a counsellor, we are just going to move you to a different bed."

Everything was a blur, 60 tablets, a bucket load of booze and my body just said, "Yeah give me some more, I can take whatever you can throw at me."

I was moved to a different bed, my boss said he was heading home for a few hours shut eye, he looked tired. I didn't blame him, he had already done enough just by coming out. He would be back after the counsellor had seen me and he was at the end of the phone if I needed him.

# CHAPTER TWO

# BACK FROM THE BRINK

I lay on the new bed, in a new room, drifting in and out of sleep or was I blacking out? I don't know, I didn't care.

Nurses came and went, shifts changed, handover of the suicidal nut and more prelims were taken, constantly monitored.

Around lunch time a nurse walked in holding a breath test. They wanted to know if I was sober enough to see a counsellor.

"Take one deep breath blow here."

You know the drill. I was sobering up, but the darkness was still lurking. I blew green. A call to the duty counsellor was made.

Great, a head doctor, I thought.

It's not like I hadn't seen them before. The time before though, they were no use in helping me. Why would this time be any different?

I was still laid up in the hospital bed when she arrived, the counsellor, the head doctor. This was a point of conflict within, did I let her in? That would be logical.

The darkness was telling me, "Spout some bollocks of being sorry, you'll never do it again. Then get out and do it properly."

My head was awash I didn't know what to do. My head

felt like a war was going on and I didn't know which side to back; the light or the dark. I was ushered to a private family room. You know the type you see on Casualty that the distraught family get shepherded into when a loved one has bought it. The décor was neutral, three chairs, a table with the hospital charter and a bin in the corner.

Then she began, "Hi. How are you feeling?"

She started politely with the standard line of questions. What should I do? Do I tell her about my darkness or do I let it win?

"I'm OK thanks and you?" Be polite back show her I am in control, I will be out of here quick.

"I am here because of last night, your overdose, I work for the NHS and I am here to asses you and get you the help you need."

Help, yeah right I've seen you lot before. Help, no doubt you will make notes, blame my past and then give me anti-depressants which turn me into a dribbling idiot. Then it will be nine months of not working and feeling a prick for letting my mates down. They'll banter me and some of the harsh stuff will hit deep, like being a war dodger. It won't matter though, nothing does, everything will be either OK or I will be dead.

I don't know what happened to me at that point, but something was warming me inside, maybe her smile, maybe the polite pleasant manner, she seemed genuine. Within two sentences, my good side was telling me to tell her about my world, my fears, my past, the point which had led me to attempt suicide.

She was good, but then the darkness told me to be careful, but the light was screaming, "No, let her see, maybe she is the key, maybe she can help."

Over the next hour I told her some of my story, no holds barred, but keeping the real dark reasons away, but giving her enough to realise why I had taken the tablets. At the end I thought I was starting to trust someone; all she did was sit and listen.

In the end she said, "It's OK. I can help you. I will find you the right people this time; we can sort this out together. Is there anyone you would like me to phone, your best friend or your boss? Let me explain things to them, this may be better coming from me."

She left me in the family room to go and make the call. My head was still swimming. Was she the key? Can or will she really help?

A few minutes passed before she returned, to give me the news of what people had said. My boss was on the way back, I wasn't going to be committed, I was to be set free. She handed me a leaflet with numbers of help lines, if I needed them. Again she reassured me she could and would help me get through this and I believed her. I headed back to the room and waited for my boss to pick me up.

It seemed like an age, my head was spinning from the discussion about my past, then my boss appeared. He wanted me to go me back to his place, he was going to let me crash there, so I wouldn't be alone. We left A&E and headed into the pouring rain to get the car. I wasn't in the mood to talk about me. It was easier just to give directions back to my place so I could grab some kit and go to his.

As I turned the key in the door, I was dreading what I was going to find, but everything was OK. A few dirty plates, an empty can of Guinness; nothing major.

I tidied up, mess really annoys me. It's the military inside me or so I thought. I headed up the stairs; next to my bed lay the empty pill packets.

"Oh well, maybe next time?"

I stuffed a load of clothes into a bag. I wanted out of

this place, too many memories. I started to shake, I hated this place.

"Let's go," I called.

Then, before I knew it, we were back in the rain, then the car, heading to my boss's house. He explained the family set up. I hadn't really thought about it but there was his wife and two kids to consider. I am sure the last thing they both needed was some nut job hanging around.

We talked in the car. I was positive, the darkness had gone for now. I really thought I had made a connection with the counsellor and she was going to help me. We pulled into his drive, I was nervous, I had only met his family once before and that was a brief encounter.

I looked and felt crap, the darkness was coming, no controlling it, I had to try and fight it and not let it in. We went inside, I was introduced to the family. I didn't feel embarrassed about the fact I had taken the overdose but I was embarrassed I had dragged others into it. After all, it was my problem; why should I be any more of a burden to them?

After a brew and a shower, I felt half normal, we sat, the football was on, it was a big game, Man U playing Chelsea. I didn't have to talk about anything if I didn't want to. A part of me felt I owed them an explanation but it wasn't expected of me. We talked about this and that.

It was the work side that bothered me. Was I heading back for the anti-depressants again? I tried to explain to my boss about our military head doctors and how bad they were. I had tried them before and they hadn't helped, they just gave me tablets and six months off flying which led to more grief from the guys. Between my boss and me, a plan was formed. Who had to know, who I wanted to know, and when we would tell them. It couldn't be today, that fight would have to wait until tomorrow.

I sort of slept that night not sure if it was it the drugs or the booze. I didn't care, finding sleep these days was hard. Before I knew it, it was time to get up and face the coffee.

This was the hard part, the getting up; it was easier not to. It was easier just to roll in the duvet and let the world pass me by. That was the problem the getting going; first the duvet, then out of the house. These everyday, normal tasks seemed to be a struggle and over the years it had got a lot worse.

A tap on the door, my boss with a brew, the good old English tradition, a cup of tea. He told me he had made an appointment with the Station Medical Officer for me and asked if I still want him to come along.

# CHAPTER THREE

# EXCESS BAGGAGE

I knew I needed him there as one problem with the military was the doctors were officers of rank. I wasn't intimidated but I wasn't myself and having an ally with me was a good idea. I showered and dressed and put on my uniform. It almost felt like a shield. It made me forget about the past and think what mattered was the job.

It's like a sportsman running onto the pitch; you put your game face on and focus on the game. My uniform had been my game face for 13 years. The RAF meant a lot to me, to me it was more than a job. We headed down the Medical Centre, I wasn't feeling great, but my game face was on. I knew a lot of questions were heading my way. I was about to have to cover old ground, the story of my life, the story of my attempted suicide.

My name was called, the doctor had come to reception to show us in offering a warm handshake and smile. My boss followed us in.

I can't remember how the conversation started but I can remember a lot of the details now. I had to try and make the doctor realise how much work meant to me. Stopping me flying would push me further back into the darkness. I told my story but I left details out.

I had just met this guy and I didn't trust him, yet. He sat and listened.

I explained about the time before when I had seen the military head doctors and how bad I felt they had been, that I didn't trust them or want them involved with me again. I had the leaflet from the counsellor and I mentioned I felt I could trust her and she had reassured me she could get me some help.

Then it was the doc's turn and my turn to listen. A few direct questions were thrown in my direction.

"Would I throw myself out of an aircraft?"

"No," I answered, explaining that putting on my helmet and walking to an aircraft was all that matters and that I wouldn't put the crew or the aircraft at risk.

The doctor then did something which I had never experienced before or expected. He wasn't going to ground me; he wasn't sending me back to the military specialists; he wasn't putting me on anti-depressants. However, I wasn't allowed to play with weapons, but he was happy for me to seek treatment with the NHS.

The only proviso was that I came back weekly to give him an update and, if I felt crap or hadn't slept, I would be man enough to go to my boss and not go flying that day. I nearly fell over, for the first time in my military career a doctor wanted to help. That appointment and the trust the doctor showed me, made me realise I was no longer on my own, I now had three allies, my boss, the counsellor and the Station Medical Officer. As I walked out, for the first time ever, I felt to be on the right road, the road which was going to give answers about the past. Maybe I had a future without the darkness?

It was time to bring others on board, tell them what I had done and tell them how low things had got. This was hard, it was asking people for help, no longer could I do this alone. In my heart I knew I had some good mates out there, they would help me, but the initial contact, the initial 'please help' had to come from me.

I reached for my phone and started scrolling through the phone book. I already had an initial list swimming in my head but my hands were shaking.

Could I phone these people and tell them? I had to. I dialled the first number, the phone was ringing, then I heard the voice of a friend. He always seemed happy; things were never too much trouble for him.

There was no easy way, so I just blurted it out "Mate on Saturday night I took an overdose, I wanted to die, I ended up in A&E, but I am OK, my body has shaken it off, now I need help."

The stunned silence, although expected, was a bit of a conversation killer. The reply was as good as it got, first he wanted the details, then where was I staying, who was watching out for me, but ultimately he would be there for me all I had to do was ask. That's the problem, the asking. When you are in the darkness to ask for help, to admit you are weak, is nearly impossible. We chatted for around five minutes and, in the end, I had what I needed. I had another fighter to help me get better; another friend who wanted me to be better and not wanting to end it.

All in all, I chatted to around four other friends. I didn't want it common knowledge on the squadron, so I only told who I wanted. That was until I was back in the boss's office; he wanted me to tell some others, people I didn't really know. Could I trust them?

My boss reassured me, I had to tell them, put them in the loop because these were guys who needed to know, just as an extra pair of eyes to watch over me. I told them, but it felt uncomfortable, I didn't go into details, I didn't want to, but the reasonable side of me knew they had to know, just for safety reasons at work.

The first day was the hardest, by the end of it I was drained of energy and everywhere I turned I felt as if people were watching my every move and I didn't like it. I was still staying around my boss's house, still everyone watching me. I was positive about what the doctor had said, but in some ways I could feel things starting to get me down.

I was in for a rough night. As I lay there awake with my iPod on, my head was racing, again I could feel myself not wanting to be here. I couldn't do anything about it. I had to wait things out. I had to keep control of the darkness.

I must have drifted off around 4am. I heard the household starting to wake around 7am, but I couldn't be bothered. All I wanted to do was stay there, not move, not get up, not do anything. My boss popped in with a morning brew, I didn't want it, but I had to play the game.

I had to get away and show I could be trusted. I struggled getting up, shower, shave, it was to be one of those days, but the thing that put a smile on my face was the pain. The pain in my back and kidneys was unbearable, on the doctor's pain scale I was an eight or nine and I loved it. I felt alive, the pain was horrendous obviously my body getting rid of the abuse I had thrown at it and through the pain I found life. I had one task that day, one last phone call to make, it was something I had thought about during the night, I had to phone the ex.

Around 10am, I went to make the phone call. I knew this was to be tough, when she had left on Sunday morning I knew then there was no going back, now I had to show her I wasn't in this shit state because of her.

I didn't want her to think I had taken an overdose because she had left. I dialled the number, she answered, after a few minutes of the usual pleasantries; I hit her with it, both barrels, no holding back.

"The overdose had nothing to do with you leaving, I don't want you thinking that you, of all people, should have known how close to the edge I was. Something pushed me, but it wasn't you!"

A stunned silence, I had her on the ropes.

"I know there is no going back, let the solicitors do their work, I will see you around. Take care. Bye."

I hung up not wanting or waiting for a reply; I had to get off that phone while I was in control. I felt pleased I had managed to make the call, but the realisation of failing at something, hit deep inside, I had failed at my marriage and I hated myself for it. Thoughts started to bounce around in my head, unpleasant thoughts, I had to fight, I had to keep them away. I was nothing like other people from my past.

Right on to my next task, my Wing Commander was back from leave. My flight boss had phoned him yesterday to put him in the picture and I was told I had his full support but I owed him more than that, a sit down face-to-face was called for.

I was lucky the Wing Commander had an open door policy, if he was in and wasn't busy his door was open, just knock and chat. I walked past the open door and glanced in. He was on the phone but he saw me and beckoned me in. I used the international sign to see if he wanted a tea or coffee as I knew I could be in there for a while. Another smile and a thumbs up.

I got the brews while he finished his call. Five minutes later, I was sat in his office, the 'Do Not Disturb' sign had been turned about and we both had a fresh brew. Now it was over to me, the best approach was no holds barred, no softening up, just come straight out with it.

"Sir, I know you have been told, but I wanted a face-to-face, Saturday I took an overdose. It wasn't a plea for help, I wanted to die. It's not the first time its happened but this time I want help to fight this because if there is a next time I won't wake up."

That summed it up in a sentence or two.

"OK, well what can I do to help? You have my full support and help in getting you better and whatever I or the squadron can do to help we will. Not just for you but for us too, we want you back, we want you fit. I know things have been really rough this past few years but let's get you sorted this time, let's get you better."

I wasn't stunned, I had worked for this guy for a year plus and he was a genuine nice guy, very approachable. He always seemed to keep his word I had never doubted it!

We chatted until the brews were empty about the support that my boss had already showed me. Not once did I feel pressure, I didn't have to tell him anything I didn't want him to now. By the end of the conversation, I was reassured I wasn't going to be carted off to the nut house. I wasn't going to be hung out to dry by the squadron.

The Wing Commander fully supported the decision to keep me flying and just reiterated the point, if I didn't feel up to it I was to put up my hand and not fly, for the safety of the crew and aircraft. I left the office relieved, although my head was spinning as I had brought up a few points of the past. I'd brought up a few things about what had gone on in the squadron that had contributed to my overdose. He hadn't been aware of them but now he knew. He could see why some things made me very uneasy and that when I relived the past the darkness won.

Over the next three or four days, I was up and down, the darkness kept seeping in, but I somehow managed not to let it consume me. Life was beginning to gain some normality. By the Thursday, I went home and left the relative safety of my boss's house. At first it felt strange, but I wanted to be able to shut myself away and escape from the world.

Even in the dark of my home and my head, the light wanted to start and seek answers. Why was I like this? I needed to understand why I had tried to kill myself. I began opening things, old boxes, old thoughts in my head, I had to file everything, sort everything and gain the answers I desperately sought. Every night, my boss phoned at 9pm to see if I was doing OK and he always offered me a place to stay if I felt bad.

Even though I didn't show it, it meant a lot to have access to someone who cared. I avoided phone calls from family for days; they never had helped in the past and I couldn't face them now. I needed distance. I needed space. I had to be selfish for the first time in my life. They were going to have to find someone else to turn to.

I picked up my mobile, and wrote a text "I am fine. You may not understand why, but please leave me alone, no contact, no calls, no texts. Sorry this is how it must be."

Send to: Mum, Stepfather, Stepmother, Sister and Brother.

This was like opening the flood gates, a volley of texts came back wanting answers.

Select 'Sent Items', resend the above text: again more texts wanting answers.

This went on for days. Caller ID is a godsend. I vetted my calls; deleted my answer phone messages without listening to them and every time I got a text I just re-sent my original text. Finally they got the message and left me alone. I had to start finding out what was wrong with me.

If you climb a mountain with a heavy rucksack of memories, in the end it may get overloaded and start to weigh you down. I was stuck half way up a mountain not able to take a step forward. I didn't want to fall back, so I unloaded some of the weight of my memories.

My family had to go if I was to reach the top of this mountain and gain some of my answers. I had to leave them behind. Maybe one day I will be strong enough to go back down the mountain, find them and carry them with me to the top, but for now this climb was about to get technical and hard.

No excess baggage allowed.

# CHAPTER FOUR

# DOWN ON MY KNEES

Over the next week, I was a little better.

I felt great not having family problems, some of my friends didn't understand this move but I had to do what felt right for me. I was airborne again although it felt as if a thousand eyes were watching me.

When my helicopter helmet went on and we walked for the aircraft, my game face went on and I forgot about everything. All what mattered was that crew, that aircraft, that mission. It was after one mission, we had landed, closed down the aircraft that a message was passed to me. I was to go and see my boss.

We had the usually pleasantries.

How was I? How did I feel?

Then he explained someone from the NHS counselling team had contacted him and I was to phone them. I used work's phone, it rang a few times before someone picked up. It was a bloke.

He explained who and where he was, then he asked me a few questions.

"Any more thoughts of suicide? How was flying this morning? By the way I am a pilot I fly from one of your local airfields."

Great, I wasn't feeling it with this guy anyway. My gut

was telling me I couldn't open up to a weekend puddle jumper pilot. If he was just looking for common ground this wasn't it. Despite everything my gut was telling me, the light inside me wanted to get my head sorted, get into the unopened files, the files which only open when I am hurting myself. I arranged a meet the next day, so armed with directions, I hung up.

The day seemed to get a little blurred from then. It was the darkness, it was telling me not to go. It was fighting against the light and telling me I didn't need them, we could sort it ourselves. If I keep looking I could find my own answers, I needed no one.

My head was swimming so I headed for the one place that was a constant in my life and the only place I could ever think straight and feel good about myself, the gym. I started training when I was 12 years old at a friend's gym back home; I started for reasons which will become apparent later. When I train, I push everything to the max. With me there isn't an easy session.

I often close my eyes and let the darkness flash a picture of something inside which hurts. It's then that I get the extra strength to go through the pain. I have pushed myself to bleeding and vomiting even to the point of collapse. When I am at this point where most would stop, I take is as a signal to push harder.

It shows I am not weak. No one can hurt me while I am here. Some say it's an addiction, it's the endorphin rush I get, but for me it's something else, it's the only place I can find inner peace. I have trained within 12 hours after operations, if injured I train around the body part. If I don't train for two or more days, I am consumed by the darkness, my inner strength is lost and it wins.

I was just back on an even keel, with the darkness was back in its place, when the phone went. I recognised the number. It was the counsellor again but why was he calling back so soon? I answered but I wasn't prepared.

"Hi, sorry there is no easy way of telling you this but because you are in the military and you have a facility within which to get help, we cannot help you. It is to do with money and who will pay for the sessions, I did try but …"

I had already stopped listening it was just noise. I hung up the phone, the darkness engulfed me, I wanted to be anywhere but here. I wanted to be anyone but me. I wanted to disappear and never return.

The feeling of being left to fight on my own had returned, I would have to sort this alone. I jumped in my car and raced home, not caring about the winding country lanes as I had to get back quick. The speed didn't matter and if I hit something and died, I would be at rest. No more darkness.

I was home, my head was spinning, answers were needed to questions, but I didn't know what the questions were.

Why did I believe in the hospital counsellor? Why did I trust her? Why would she want to help me?

I was feeling real bad. My eyes went to the beer fridge, then the wine rack, now the spirit cupboard. Maybe a little beer will take the edge off? Fortunately I must have had an angel on my shoulder trying to subdue the darkness.

"Come on let's sort this, there are others that can help, don't do it."

A struggle went on all night. With the stereo on random, I just sat all night, not really listening, not really doing anything. Every time I was thirsty, I got a coffee, tea or water, anything but alcohol. The light had won this round.

The next day, I was programmed to fly but I was a wreck. I had not been to bed, not slept at all, now it was time to be man enough to tell them I was unfit. I entered my boss's office, I didn't need to speak.

He saw it in my eyes, "Close the door, do you want to talk about it?"

I sat down and told him of yesterday's events, he too felt betrayed by these people who also had reassured him I was going to get help. I was off the flight and I was to see the doctor.

I got down to the docs as soon as he was free, again the warm handshake, again the understanding, then he told me how far I had come.

"Just over a week ago, you would have taken that drink and had another. Then who knows? We can sort this."

He sensed my desolation and continued, "Don't worry, I am not sending you to Brize if you don't want to go. Let's see what we can come up with. We'll try the Internet, see what's available privately. There will be a cost but it will be worth it."

We sat and chatted for around 20 minutes. I told him about ditching my family and again he thought this was another positive move, another step in the right direction. I started to like this guy, maybe he can really help. He seems genuine. He hasn't just ditched me or sent me to the military head doctors who would just put me straight on the dribbling idiot tablets again and stop me flying.

I made an appointment to see him again in a couple of days, he then showed me my notes on the computer screen and asked me if I was happy with what he had written about me. I was taken back, there was no negative, no details, just he had advised me about private help. Now I knew I could trust him, not only had he kept me flying, not only had he not sent me to our head doctors, he wasn't stabbing me in the back. My notes would follow me around the RAF and he wanted to make sure I was happy with what was in them.

When I returned to work, my boss was waiting, wanting to know what the doctor had said; he then invited me around to his for a meal. I think he didn't want me to go back to the house and to be honest I didn't want to go back either. My head had had enough today. Just one thing left to do, the gym.

The session was hard, mainly due to being so tired from having no sleep, but even being tired was no excuse for having a half-arsed session, I still pushed the boundaries just to feel that bit of pain, that bit of normality.

I went for dinner; it was nice and relaxed; no pressure from anyone. It was when my boss was putting his youngest to bed, that his wife and I had a heart to heart. She had always been nice to me, it must have been hard to meet me just after the overdose, but something inside me told me, she might understand what was going on. I told her bits and pieces; the duvet days; the not wanting to get up; the constant inner battle between the light and the dark. I was thankful she understood.

I didn't know much about their lives but something told me she had dealt with hard times as well. I then told her how disappointed I was with the NHS and how alone I felt, she suggested something which I had never heard of before called homeopathy.

Call me ignorant but I hadn't a clue what she was on about but she started to try to explain the concept to me.

"Well, it's kind of herbal or alternative therapy. What a homeopath does is, they get to the root cause of the problem, strip away all the bad and start fixing the core. It's like an onion, they peel back the layers until they find the heart and then they repair the heart and help put back on the layers in a more manageable order. I have a friend who is a trainee maybe I can give her a call if you would like to try it. She may use you as a final case study for her exams if you wish."

I thought about it, herbal, alternative medicine, sounds

a bit hippy to me, but I remembered my Gran, she is a firm believer of the old herbal remedies. When she had recommended them in my past they all seemed to work. So what had I to lose?

"Well, I am not sure I have ever heard about it, do they have a website where I can research it, before I commit?"

No sooner had I asked than she was on the phone to her friend the trainee, and I was given a web address so I could do my own research. I began to feel I was moving in the right direction to leave the darkness and find some answers. What had made me like this? I had to know.

The next day I did my research and I liked what I found. It isn't like someone can wake up and decide to become a homeopath. It takes years to qualify. I read the pros and cons and reports from people who believed and didn't.

I felt compelled to make a decision but I was just getting myself confused. I'd researched a more conventional counsellor in the local area, this was a nightmare there were hundreds. It was impossible to tell what was good or bad. I didn't understand some of the names of the therapies. I started to get frustrated. Why was I doing it? Why should I care if I get fixed or not? Who gives a damn?

Before I knew it, it was back; the darkness was here again.

I grabbed my rucksack filled it up so it weighed around 40 pounds. It was time to punish myself, time to feel pain. Next, the running shoes were on and I was off.

It was ice cold outside but it didn't matter, I had to run, escape this place and escape myself. I set off, before I knew it I was well into the country lanes with innumerable blind corners. I longed for a car to race around a corner and hit me, take my darkness away. I felt alone, frustrated and I badly wanted help, but no one was giving it to me.

I found myself on a single track road. It was getting

near dusk, just the time when drivers are heading home feeling dull from their days' work. I saw the car half a mile away, I just kept my head down and kept going, I was in the middle of the road, the car was coming towards me and I didn't care. He saw me at the last minute and slammed on his brakes. I could even hear the sound of his ABS working hard.

It stopped short and I just ran around it. I glanced into the car, the driver was as white as a sheet. It was a close call. If he only knew how disappointed I was he hadn't hit me. I ran for miles more until my legs and lungs were bursting from the cold air. I felt pain in my back so I stopped took off my rucksack and felt into the small of my back.

My hand was red with blood. My rucksack had rubbed me raw and now I was bleeding. This pleased me. I knew I had gone through the pain, time to head home. Getting going again was a struggle though as the rucksack kept rubbing the same spot. I felt the pain but it kind of felt normal. I enjoyed the feeling and had gained some satisfaction, so much so that the run home was long but uneventful.

At home I cleaned the wound. The TCP stung my back like hell but the pain didn't bother me. It was time to head back to the research, time to try to find help and find an answer. I read deep into the night, looking for an opening, looking for the right person to help me. The thing I kept returning to was homeopathy. Maybe it could just work. Maybe this was the help I desperately needed and wanted.

The next day I was in pain from both the wound on my back and severely swollen knees. This just made me more positive I was in my light, I had decided that I would try homeopathy.

I headed back to the doctor, I told him, what I had decided and asked him his opinion. I cannot really remember what he said but, in essence, it was to give it a go. I didn't mention the run the night before or the wound on my back. Best not push his boundaries too hard for now. I knew I could trust him, but something inside my head told me to keep it to myself.

The week then flew by and I had heard nothing. It was the weekend before I knew it. They were the worst. I was rattling around the house, trying to keep myself busy, trying not to think too much. I kept going to the gym or running. I just needed to tire myself out to make my brain stop thinking.

I realised that was why I enjoyed work so much. When I got to fly there was no way I could think about me as others were more important.

The weekend passed in a blur. I hadn't hit the bottle since the overdose, I was trying hard not to take the easy path. This time I wanted answers. I had such a burning desire to find out what was wrong with me.

Soon Monday morning had arrived and my boss had good news from his wife. I was to call in after work.

She had contacted her friend, the homeopath, and told her a little about me. Although she wanted to help me, the homeopath was worried about using me as a case study, as she didn't want to get it wrong. If the darkness won, next time that could be it. Fair enough who would want that on their conscience?

So even though she didn't want to take me on, she had left me details of someone she knew who had been practicing for years. I was given a number to call.

My nature is one of wanting things sorted there and then, this time like all the times of my past it was up to me, I had to make the call.

That night I went running again but this time it was icy and dark in the back lanes. My knees were still weak and it was almost inevitable that I slipped.

I felt my knee pop. It had twisted outwards and I was sprawled on the floor in a crumpled heap.

"Bollocks!"

I picked myself up and took a tentative step but the pain shot through the knee. They hadn't been right for years since a helicopter accident and I knew I was miles from home, only one thing for it. I closed my eyes only for images of the past to flood my head. So I opened my eyes and ran. The pain in my head was far worse than the knee. As soon as I got back I iced and elevated it but I knew it was a mess.

The next day I hobbled into work.

"Sorry boss, I fell last night, my knee is busted."

I made an appointment for the doc, but my usual couldn't see me. The last thing I wanted was awkward questions from someone different. I wasn't ready for that today.

The locum I saw was a runner. He just said to rest it and not to run for six weeks. He gave me an anti-inflammatory and stopped me from flying for the next two weeks before sending me on my way. There were no questions about the past it was the only bonus.

I was hobbling around work, made even more difficult as I had to negotiate three flights of stairs. It didn't take long before I was bored with it as now I really couldn't do a lot. I kept drifting in and out of my darkness now the distraction of flying was gone.

Best I go to the gym. I trained hard, the frustration was great, I pushed and pushed I felt it welling up inside me. I found myself heading for the loos, just as I was closing the door, I vomited. I was glad I had pushed myself. I wouldn't let the knee hold me back. My light had once again started to seep in.

But the darkness came back with a vengeance when I got home even though I was in constant pain, which was good. I was heading back into the darkness; the momentary glimpse of light when I was puking was just a flash. I knew I couldn't work and I hated it.

What was left? So I turned the stereo on, opened a bottle of wine.

"Fuck it! What harm can one bottle do?"

I didn't care. I sat down in front of the speakers and listened to Bon Jovi full blast. Some of their songs had helped me out in the past, but not this time.

I sat there drinking one glass then another in the darkness, no lights on, just the light from the stereo display. I saw my reflection in the patio doors.

"Is this what I had become?"

I poured another glass, the past was in my head.

"Why me? Why me? Why me? What had I done?"

The darkness was back, darker than ever. I opened another bottle without thinking. I sat and listened with the stereo on random. Some music helped, some didn't. It was late into the night; I had sat for a couple of hours and another bottle was emptied.

Before I knew it I was on to the Jack Daniels and Dry.

I headed into the bathroom cupboard. I looked at the pill box, it was empty, I had thrown everything out after last time.

I was in a dark place, but not yet dark enough, I wasn't in the mood for killing myself. I closed my eyes, images, feelings of the past.

"Stop!" The light side came into my head, "Let's sort this."

I had to listen so I put on the kettle. Time for coffee, time to listen to the light side. I sat all night in front of the stereo.

When dawn came I knew I couldn't face the outside world today. I just wanted to be on my own. I was still in a semi-dark place. I had a desire to leave me behind, leave my wallet on the side, leave the car in the garage, pack a few clothes and head off. Run away.

I texted a work colleague to tell him I hadn't slept and wouldn't be coming in. I just had to find some answers.

I headed for the spare room where a lot of my history was stored. I emptied the bookshelf, looking at old photos, reading old letters.

I was searching desperate to find an understanding, nothing was here, nothing was giving me an understanding. All it was doing was making me darker, I hated me, I hated my past.

I headed to the garage next and found my saviour. My push bike was set up on my indoor trainer so I jumped on clicked my feet in the pedals and began to spin. The pain in my knee was a kindly reminder that I was still alive.

I stopped for a while and sat and thought. The day my dad died, I sat here in this very spot and cycled for four hours.

Why was I smiling about that? Was it the fact I cycled for four hours or was it that this was the only way I knew how to deal with my head?

My knee was burning with pain so I upped the cadence and was turning the pedals harder, faster. Sweat was flowing off me like a river. I puked. The pain was too much for my body.

"Keep going, don't quit."

I was sick again and again, but every time I just upped the cadence and resistance. When it was too hard, I closed my eyes and let a painful memory in.

"Right, keep going."

If I was fit and strong nothing could harm me. Eventually my body gave up and there was vomit and sweat everywhere. I unclipped, satisfied with my effort and headed to bed. Tomorrow was another day, I knew I would sleep through. No nightmares as I was physically and mentally exhausted.

This was my strategy to stop being haunted by dreams of the past.

# Chapter Five

# Homeopathy

The next day I was ready to go back to work. I knew I couldn't fly but I needed to get out of the house and get a little human contact. I had been alright and I had slept through with no nightmares and no waking up.

The day proved uneventful. I found explaining myself to friends about the knee. It was good they could see a physical injury; only a few knew the mental injury I was carrying.

Around lunch time, I caught up with my boss. He asked me what happened yesterday and I told him I hadn't slept and struggled to leave the house. He asked me if I had contacted the homeopath his wife's friend had recommended. I told him I hadn't.

After a northern pep talk, he made it clear to me it was time. I was quite nervous, I went outside to get a better signal on my mobile phone. I typed in the homeopath's number, pressed call, then I hung up.

A voice in my head was questioning it. Did I need her? Was it a good idea? It was the darkness.

I tried again, this time I let it ring, but put it down again. If she was home she probably now thought she had some weirdo phoning her. I had to get a grip and take the plunge. This could mean me getting better but did I want to, that the question? Did I need her help?

I should be strong enough to do this alone. "Come on let's sort this," the light side kept telling me. I rang again this time I left it ringing, an answer phone picked up. She wasn't there. A message, I must leave a message, so I left my name and number and how I had been given her number then put the phone down. My head was spinning, I was questioning why I needed someone and if I had done the right thing. One voice was telling me it was good, the other was bad, only one thing for it the gym.

I had only left the gym 10 minutes when I felt my phone vibrate in my pocket. I checked the display and recognised the number, it was the homeopath.

"Hi, you left me a message to call you, how can I help?"

I explained, "I was given your number from a friend of a friend in the village, she is a trainee homeopath and wasn't sure if she could help me. Apparently I need someone with a little more experience, so I thought I would call and give you a try."

I was trying to seem relaxed, but inside I was burning up, my inner darkness was wanting me to just hang up, drop the phone and forget I ever had her number.

"Well, I don't know the person who gave you my number but I am a fully qualified homeopath and can make you an appointment to see me either at my home or one of my clinics. Which would suit you best?"

I was thinking about trying to stay anonymous. I have a very distinctive car and I didn't want it to be seen outside the clinic in the village. People would talk, nothing is every private.

"Err, your home will be fine, when can I see you?" I replied.

"How about Monday afternoon, shall we say about 1pm? I will give you some directions as I live in the country and you may find it hard to find. Also I will post something out to you ; hopefully it will reach you before Monday but don't worry about it if it doesn't. Have you got a pen?"

I jotted down the directions, they seemed complicated but I wouldn't know until I was on the ground. I would get there early and check the lay of the land so I wouldn't be late. Punctuality was one good discipline the military had installed in me. The conversation came to a close with the usual pleasantries of "I look forward to meeting you." To be honest I wasn't, I was dreading it.

I walked back in the Squadron, my head wasn't there. I headed for the planning room, to find where it was I had to go. I checked the local maps, but couldn't put my finger on it. I recognised the name of the village but could I find it? A mate walked by so I asked him if he knew where it was, we both pored over a map but the place still eluded us. My mate then called over someone else who was working in the planning room; now three of us pored over the map; everyone was trying to help. Lucky for me n0-one asked me why I had to go there.

Eventually we came across the village and it wasn't too far. I estimated 45 minutes, but I would give myself a good hour and a quarter for my first run. The next task finding my boss to see about getting the Monday off. I knew it wouldn't be a problem but there are channels to go through, even if you are a nut job. I was right, time off wasn't a problem, I could have as much as I need to get better. It went on the planning board and I was entered as having a meeting and to see the boss for further details, so if anyone looked they would have to go through him. With everything squared away for Monday. I decided to head to the gym. I still was grounded due to my knee, it was no better, but I needed my fix, so for the second time that day I headed for my safe place, the gym.

By the time I got home I was shattered, the last couple of days had finally taken their toll. I made myself a snack, food had taken on a new meaning these days. I only ate because I knew I had to. I had to feed my muscles or I wouldn't have energy to fight. No longer was it a pleasure to eat but a necessary evil. My bed was looming rapidly, hopefully I could sleep, but as soon as I hit the pillow, I was awake. Thoughts and feelings just going around and around, I knew I had another restless night ahead.

The rest of the week was just the same mundane life. Get up, go to work, go to the gym, eat, lie in bed. I had lost the drive for answers and was falling back into existence only. Inside I knew it was wrong, but I had put Monday on a pedestal, this was a chance for help. I was worried about going, it was a big step but it was a chance I had to take. Inside I had mixed feelings, some hours I was up for it and others there was no way on earth I was going.

Sunday night like most nights was restless; I still had doubts about what lay ahead. When I awoke the next morning, I tried to keep busy by checking my route on the AA's website time and again. I looked for alternatives if one road was blocked. How I could divert and how long a diversion would take me?

Minutes seemed like hours, hours like days. I kept making a brew, but kept putting it down somewhere, while I popped off to do some little niggly job. Anything to keep me busy and take my mind off the appointment. By the time I got back to my brew, it was cold, so I would head into the kitchen and make a fresh cup. This went on all morning.

The time eventually came. I had the route, a full tank of petrol, my favourite music loaded into the multi-disk. I was off. I was sleep driving, before I knew where I was I was nearly there; not knowing how I had got there or if it had been a busy journey. I was having to tell myself to switch on now the roads were becoming unfamiliar. I was driving with the route on my knee, next roundabout right, then straight over the one after that, keep on this road for five miles. I saw a signpost for the village I was heading for. I felt my heart rate begin to elevate as I knew I was getting near. Before I knew it, I was in the village. I had made it with a good half an hour to spare so I pulled into a public car park knowing the private road I needed was just off to the left.

I turned off the engine and grabbed my hill jacket, it was a wet grey December day. My skin is waterproof but I didn't want to turn up wet and flustered for my first meeting. I walked for a while as fortunately the car park was the start of a local beauty spot. It was nice but I really didn't pay that much attention to what lay around me, I just made notes of what cars were about. Were there any curtains moving or any faces at windows? There was no one else around the car park. Obviously the weather had put the ramblers off or maybe it was just Monday.

As I walked, all I could think about was what was about to happen. I was feeling scared, I didn't want to go, one side of my head was telling me not to bother but the other side was telling me I had to go. I kept checking my watch; I still had to find the house. Best I head back to the car and dry off a little, the car windows steamed up instantly. I couldn't have looked more suspicious. I pushed the start button, the engine fired into life, selected first gear and then headed for the single-tracked private road; it was steep and twisty as had been described to me a few days earlier.

A couple of houses were on the hillside and looked expensive. When I got to the top, there was a sign for three houses. I turned right by the neighbour's tennis court. What was I letting myself in for?

Again I followed the twisty road around, then a stunning house came into view. What looked to be a workshop stood to the right of the drive with wood chippings near the entrance. A VW van was parked outside, to the left of it a VW estate. I reverse parked opposite so if I needed to leave in a hurry I could. My palms were sweaty even in the cold and my heart was thumping in my chest. I just sat trying to compose myself for the walk to the door.

I closed my eyes. Come on think, find the strength, here is an opportunity to sort things. I opened the door and stepped back out into the rain. There appeared to be no one in the workshop, I heard nothing. I headed for the door, I looked for a bell, there wasn't one, but a brass door knocker in the middle stood proud. I reached out, my hands shaking, I tapped three times, then I stood back and waited trying to compose myself. The door opened, a lady stood there with a warm smile.

"Hi is it Matt? Please come in out of the rain."

She held out her hand; she must have felt how sweaty and nervous I was. I stepped into a wooden hallway, to the right a kitchen, in front a set of stairs.

"Please come through, can I get you a glass of water?"

"Err, yes please, that would be nice."

"Matt go to the left and make yourself at home."

I entered a sitting room with two cream three-seater couches in the middle divided with a coffee table. To the right, a cabinet with lots of little potion bottles in, below this was a desk lots of paperwork, an answer phone and an Apple notebook sat blinking on standby. There was a wood-burning fire crackling in the hearth, a piano in one corner. Then lots of photos, obviously pictures of the family, lay all around the room.

I noticed no TV and no stereo, this was obviously a room to relax in. I looked out of the patio doors to a wonderful view over the valley and the village I had just driven through. I recognised the view as I had flown around here many times.

She soon came back into the room holding two glasses of water, still smiling.

"It's a better view when the sun is shining, please take a seat. Did you find it OK? It does get a little twisty in places," she said. "Please forgive me today I have the sniffles I was thinking over the weekend I may have had to reschedule today, but I picked up yesterday and from what I have been told, you need a little help sooner rather than later."

I sat across from her facing the door so I could see if anyone else was moving around the house. The coffee table housed the two glasses of water, she held a clipboard with a piece of paper waiting to take notes.

"Before we start can you tell me a little more about homeopathy? I researched it on the Internet, but what is the training and ethos? Is everything I say between us like a doctor and patient?

"Yes, everything you say to me is between us. I take notes so I can review your case, no one else has access to them. I trained in London at the Society for Homeopaths for five years before I was fully qualified and registered so you cannot just wake up one day and decide to become a homeopath. Homeopaths have been around for centuries, we believe that to fix a person we need to get to the core and fix this using a remedy."

She could see the relief coming over my face and continued, "Not everyone's remedy is the same and we have remedies for everything. It's a case of finding the right one when we get to know each other. I will start to think about one which I think would be right for you, we try it and see what happens."

She must have seen the cynic in my face and went on, "Sometimes you get it right first time, sometimes it takes a couple of goes. I will consult my books and laptop and look at the different advantages of each remedy and then I will give you one to take either on a little sugar tablet or with a dropper."

I asked, "Do you have any ties to the military? It's just I need to be able to be away from them to allow me to sort things out. I only found you through a friend of a friend and I still am a little unsure."

She smiled and said, "Regarding the military thing, the only contact I have with them is when you fly over my house. My dad use to be a pilot so I understand a little of ranks and the structure of the RAF, but I will not contact them about you unless you ask me too. I don't even know your friend's friend. She did phone me and tell me a little about you and she was right if it is her final year of study she doesn't want to mess you about. So she contacted me to see if I had a spot, I juggled things about and here we are. As I said what is said to me stays with me, the notes are for my reference only."

Her answers settled me a little.

"I saw some military doctors a couple of years ago about depression, they were only interested in the last few years and I never could open up to them, tell them about the real truth and the real darkness that drives me on. I need help, I cannot keep going like I am tired, I have no fight left in me. I was scared to come clean with them, they put me on anti-depressants straight away and stopped me flying. I love to fly. Being free is everything and when I put on my helmet it all goes away for a while but it is always there when I get back. My doctor now has been a godsend, he trusts me."

"Why do you think he trusts you?" she said.

I replied, "After what I did he could have sent me away but he didn't. He kept me going and now I have found you.

I am here now because of him and it's taken some guts. I wasn't going to come, this is quite scary. I don't know you. I know I have to tell you things so you can help. Maybe I am looking for an answer, a magic pill, some hope to hold onto. I hope you can help."

She paused and thought about her answer, "It's OK Matt. You're here now and have taken the first step. I don't know about a magic pill, but I will try my best to heal you. I need to know everything, don't be embarrassed. Tell me everything, there are no ranks here, there are no connections. I won't stop you flying or judge you. I am here to help so why don't you start right at the beginning?"

I drew breath, both voices in my head chattering away, do I tell her? What did I have to lose?

Over the next few weeks, I sat and told her my whole story. She was the first person I have told everything to. It was muddled and confusing as I kept skipping from one time to another, depending on what popped into my head at the time.

I found with her I could talk and talk. She sat patiently and made notes. Never once did she check the time. It was supposed to be an hour long session. When I opened the floodgates to my head I couldn't close them, it just kept going. The first session lasted well over 2 hours, it just all kept coming out.

Eventually there was nothing left. I was drained but relieved. After all the sessions my homeopath had to spend a lot of time piecing my past together, putting the events in chronological order.

I thought everything had come out in that first session but over the next weeks and months more things appeared in my head, things I hadn't thought about for many a year, I told her everything in the end, I wanted to be better. I wanted to be normal and be rid of my darkness.

So how did a big, strong man, with years of military training, get reduced to a nervous wreck? I needed answers; I needed some space back in my head, it felt full, no room to move or breathe. Was it going to be this simple? Did I just need to tell someone my story from the beginning to the end?

# CHAPTER SIX

# BLOOD ON THE TRACKS

My first childhood memories are pretty normal ones. I lived in a semi in a village near Holmfirth with my mum, dad and older sister. Holmfirth is a small town that sits just north of the Peak District in West Yorkshire. There were woods and fields all around to play in and have childhood adventures.

Dad seemed to work long hours but we saw him at the weekend. Mum took care of us as well as helping my Grandma and Granddad at their pub in the neighbouring village.

It was on a trip into the woods with my family that I got my first taste of real pain. Boys will be boys. I had found a fallen branch half hanging off a tree, it called me to climb it. Getting up was OK but getting down was a problem.

As it turned out, I found the quick way by slipping and I landed on my back; knocking the wind clean out of me. How I didn't break something I don't know. I remember the struggle for breath and my eyes watering. My mum ran up the path to where I lay. She was in a panic which caused me to panic too. When you have no breath in your body it just makes things worse. Fortunately my Grandma was there and, as an ex-nurse, she calmed the situation down. Before I knew it, I was on my feet and we all were heading for my Grandma's house to have a recovery cup of tea and some homemade cake.

Life use to be so simple.

I had just turned five years old, and had only been at school since Easter, when I got to see my first dead body. It was while Mum was working in the pub and we were at my Grandma's house next door, on my first summer holiday.

Near to where we lived there was a secure mental institute. From time to time, the inmates escaped and alarms sounded and the emergency services set out looking for the loon that had beat the system and had got out. We knew someone had escaped because Grandma had made us stay inside the house.

Lots of police cars and an ambulance arrived at the railway station and we were herded inside. Something had happened on the railway line. After an hour of trying to see out of the window, I snuck outside. There was a breeze block wall designed to stop anyone falling down the railway embankment but a great place to view what was going on and not to be seen.

That's when I saw it. It was being carried by ambulance men and police, on a stretcher. It had a cover on that was going red in places, then someone ran up and put an arm which had swung down back under the cover. It didn't seem real, just an adventure. It didn't occur to me that at some point that thing had life in it. I overheard later that the escapee had jumped off the railway bridge to end it all. Even at the age of five, I remember wondering what made him do it and what his story was.

It was this summer too that things first started to go wrong. We spent time at Grandma's whilst Mum worked. The pub was having work done to it and it was an adventure playground. Big piles of soil to climb. Mini diggers moving things; builders who seemed to take an interest in anything except the job in hand, including a young boy like me.

One of the labourers took an extra interest in me. I never saw him talking to Mum but he let me sit in the digger and pull the lever's to get the bucket to dump soil. I was in childhood heaven, playing in a digger, this guy nothing seemed to be too much trouble for him. Later I was to find out why.

The mornings flew by. Every day I found my new friends and every afternoon we would head home with Mum and play in the cul-de-sac. We played for hours with marbles.

During one such game we dropped some marbles into a neighbour's garden. There was only one way into the garden without been seen from the neighbours front window, we had to go through the electrical substation next door. The older kids jumped the wall to start a search. I was keeping watch in the electrical substation, when the back door opened, I shouted "RUN!".

We all fled, but I lost my footing on the gravel by the substation and fell. It hurt, but the older kids came back not afraid of the neighbour. After all they knew who we were, I suppose if we just went and knocked on the door they would have let us collect our marbles. I had lots of pain in my shoulder, we sat on the railway bridge for a while, I was still in pain but we had to get our stories straight. We couldn't go home and tell our parents that we were in someone's garden. More importantly, we were in the substation and we knew that was illegal even if we weren't aware of the full dangers at that age.

It was decided that I had tripped over the kerb edging whilst charging about. I was taken back home, still in lots of pain. The pain didn't stop all night and the next day I was taken to casualty. Then I had my first x-ray to find I had fractured my collar bone. That put an end to any further adventures that summer. I was facing six weeks having my arm in a sling. The rest of the summer just passed away.

The new term at school had started and I remember going through the motions of school. My memories seem to come and go about the time I was there. I was always happiest by myself. The school didn't like this, I was "odd" wanting to be alone. My parents were called to discuss me; it wasn't for bad behaviour, but for being alone. I remember being made to stand under the clock. This is where all the naughty kids were sent. I never understood what had I done wrong. The meeting finished, I was told I had to make more of an effort with others and make friends.

My head was so full of adventures why did I need others? I had to do as I was told my Dad had come home from work early and didn't seem best pleased by it. My adventures and my imagination had to be controlled; I didn't want to upset my Dad.

I remember the walk to school was uphill and the way home was down. Out of school, I ran full pelt down the lane, stopping just before the main road. This had a metal fence to stop us running straight into the road. I would then turn left and there was the crossing lady, over the zebra crossing, wait at another junction, then the crossing lady took us across this road, in front was the old youth club. It was once a grand building but now run down; a big old place with yet more metal railings. Just to the side of this was the Co-op and outside there was a bench where Mum would be waiting. She then walked me and my sister down the next roads all downhill to our cul-de-sac next to the railway station. That was my after school routine.

This happened day after day and then one day, Mum was waiting with the builder from the pub. He was the one who had let me play in the digger in the summer. Mum was looking a little upset, she said she had something to tell us both and we had to be brave. We weren't going to be seeing Dad for a while. We were all going to be living in a new house and we would be going to a new school.

In those days divorces were few and far between. It wasn't a common play ground topic that's for sure. All I knew was I wasn't going home, what about my Dad? My toys? I was confused. We got into the car. In some ways it felt like a mini adventure, but I didn't really know what was happening. My sister who is two years older than me may have known a little more but she wasn't saying.

We arrived at his house. It was on the main road going to Huddersfield, there were fields behind us. It seemed bigger than our old house, although the bathroom was downstairs. He had a dart board hanging on one wall in the dining room. We were taken upstairs to our new bedroom.

There were three bedrooms. One wasn't used and stored stuff. One was for Mum and her new boyfriend and one for me and my sister. I was put out, I didn't have my own room and I was to share with my sister. There was another door which had another little room but it was tiny. Downstairs there were two living rooms both with coal fires, kitchen, bathroom and a cellar. The cellar seemed to hold something I didn't want to see. It was a place never to enter. Another adventure I kept in my head.

The next few weeks were spent settling in to a new school and even more new adventures. As we hadn't seen Dad for a while, my sister and I knew this was to be our new home. To help us settle in we were taken on walks around the fields. It was on one of these walks that he took us to this viaduct, three fields behind us. It was impressive, a scramble up the banking side and we were on a disused railway line, but on the viaduct I never got the feeling of being alone. Hairs on the back of my neck stood on end; things were strange up there. I never could put a finger on it, was my imagination running wild again?

Weeks passed and we were introduced to different people but still no Dad. It was all confusing and upsetting. We eventually did meet up though at Grandma's house for Sunday lunch. It was good to see him; he tried to explain the last few weeks but I didn't care. It was just nice having Dad around again. Things started to stabilise we started seeing Dad regularly on a weekend. The next couple of years were like this before things started to take a turn for the worse.

We moved yet again. An inheritance of a substantial amount of money was left to Mum's new partner. They decided to buy my Grandma's and Granddad's old house in a neighbouring village. That meant another change of schools and further new friendships needed to be formed.

I still found this difficult to do. What was the point? We would only move soon. At least if my adventures from my head included just me, there was no way of being let down. The divorce had been well finalised and I cannot remember my Mum re-marrying, but she did and soon fell pregnant. Dad had started re-building too and we were introduced to the woman who would soon become his second wife. She was Dad's secretary from work who was quite a few years younger but seemed OK. At home, my life had taken its first tumble when my Mum's new husband started showing his true colours. If he had a beer he got angry, not at us but he just got nasty. I never knew why. My brother was born and attention was then taken away from my sister and me. We were left to do our own thing.

My unhappiness started to spill into school. I don't know why I felt unhappy, I just did, this led to poor concentration. I would stare blindly not listening, lost in my own thoughts. One day, I was doing an exercise in the classroom, I presented my workbook to the teacher, she asked me to do some minor corrections and I saw red a little voice inside said, "Rip it, go on let it all out!"

I shook with anger and then I ripped the book up in front of her, ripping it to shreds, not caring what the consequences might be. The whole class stopped and stared in total disbelief at what they had just seen, they couldn't believe what I just had done. I didn't care, I was punished. The teacher tried to find out why I had done it and asked me what was wrong? I just went inside; I didn't know what was wrong, I couldn't answer her. The lunch bell rang and we all went for lunch, I was still upset and angry. During lunch the headmaster said something to me and all I did was ignore him, he got angry at me, so I mocked him by sticking out my tongue. He took me by the scruff of my neck, ripping me out of my seat, again I didn't care. At the time, physical punishment was still allowed so he was entitled to beat me. He used a slipper, whacking me several times before throwing me into the corridor, and making me stand with my nose to the wall in front of everyone, to think about what I had done. Despite tears and sobs, I wouldn't let him win, I withdrew into myself; my head was safe because nothing could hurt me here.

When Dad married again his company gave him a truly great wedding gift and made him redundant. It was during the depression of the 80s, Thatcher's legacy, when times were hard for most people. The loss of his job, and not being able to find another, cost him the family home and he was forced to move away from the area. This meant the regular weekend visits ended. Every three to four weeks we would go to Grandma's for Sunday dinner Dad and his new wife would spend several hours getting there by bus.

Every Sunday would be the same, Granddad, Dad and his wife would leave for the local pub and Grandma would take us for a walk. When the pub closed, they would return for dinner. As Granddad was always worse for wear, the teasing and tormenting would begin. First, the Chinese arm burns and if I sobbed, I would be teased for been soft like a little girl. Although he thought it was all in good fun, sometimes he forgot his limits. A veteran from the war, he was a tough old guy. It was always upsetting to say goodbye knowing it would be three to four weeks before we would see everyone again.

Returning to Mum's house, more teasing and tormenting would begin, this time from Mum's husband, this time it wasn't playful. On one particular Sunday we returned to find that the glass had been smashed in the living room door. Mum explained that his sister had died; she had been in a mental institution after she watched her Father die in a boating accident. He had seen red, probably with a bellyful of booze and smashed the door, Mum looked and sounded scared.

It was after this incident I started to really pick up on what was happening. Mum tried her best to shelter us from it, but she could never truly do so. We had to move again, more upheaval. Back to his old house from before; this led to yet another new school. My sister and I spent longer caring for my brother as this year's new venture was a milk round. This meant Mum and her husband were either up and out early, asleep in the afternoon or out until late. We were spending more time away from home, time at family friends or holidays at Grandma's caravan in the little seaside town of Knott End-on-Sea. This was superb as there were several places to explore and I could do it alone.

I know why Mum sent us away a lot. It wasn't that she didn't care, she was scared. I remember her wrists being bandaged, I never knew why until a few years later when someone let it slip. There was a lot of anger in the house, fuelled by booze, but even sober her husband had his violent moments. We were scared. Mum's story is hers to tell, the violence increased and with it the fear for all of us.

He shifted his anger at times. Dad always phoned on a Thursday night and it would upset me. I hated where I was as I could feel things around me going wrong and I was too weak to change it. It was one of these occasions I came off the phone, to be mocked and a box of tissues bounced off my head. I started to really hate this guy. My sister was constantly upset too, both her and Mum were scared. I wanted to help be strong for everyone, protect them from him. I hated seeing people scared so I started to hate myself for not being able to do anything about it.

One day my sister was really upset and I tried to comfort and reassure her, "Don't worry I'll take him he cannot hurt us, I won't let him. I'll take him down."

Brave words, but anything to try and help her feel better. We were in the kitchen, he was there, he said something to my sister and it was time I showed him. I screamed at him to have a go at me instead of her if he was such a tough man. He did. I was picked up by the neck and flung 15 feet across the kitchen into the wall. I cried out, it hurt, I stood up and raced out. I had to run, I didn't know where, all I knew was I had to go. I was three fields away, my heart beating fast I was terrified that he was coming after me, before me was the viaduct. I scrambled up the banking and I was at the top in quick time, despite the loneliness and feelings of not being alone up there. I could see the house and finally I began to calm down, as nobody had come after me. I shook, angry, upset, I was useless, I needed out. A few hours later I returned home for no other reason than I didn't know what else I could do.

Soon after this, Dad and his wife returned to the area and I jumped at the opportunity to go and live with them on a full-time basis. It upset Mum but I needed to get away from her husband. I had to go and leave my Mum, sister and my stepbrother behind, I was too weak to stop him.

# CHAPTER SEVEN

# THE DARE

Life seemed pretty good at Dad's house. The house was small, downstairs a tiny kitchen and a living room diner with a fireplace, impressive stone work around the edge, upstairs, three adequate bedrooms all heated by a single gas heater at the top of the stairs. The house was always cold, winter saw frost on the inside of the windows. Even in summer, some rooms were colder than others and you never felt alone. Was my imagination running away with me again?

It wasn't plain sailing but he at least was glad to have me around. His wife was a different matter entirely. She didn't have children of her own, it was new to her; how to deal with a nine year old.

She needed to be more understanding and flexible, but she insisted on treating me like I was about four. I got tired of her really quickly, she wasn't my Mum. I needed her to back away as she was reminding me of Mum's husband. The same but different; I didn't know how, I just did. I wasn't allowed any freedom, after coming from a home where I was free to explore the fields and could go to bed when I wanted, I wasn't allowed to do anything, it was too overpowering for me. The only freedom I managed was the bus journey to school; it gave me a welcome break from her constant rules and discipline.

In the March of my last year of primary school I was picked to represent the school's football team. I was playing out of position and had a shocking game, people laughed at me. My Dad and his wife were on the sidelines, she seemed to laugh the most. I was substituted after the first half. When we headed home, they went to the local and I ended up eating junk food. Later that night I was constantly ill, the next day I was worse, I couldn't move, I was bent double with pain, nothing stayed down, all she could do was blame the junk food.

The next day Dad headed for work but told his wife to get me an appointment at the doctors as soon as possible, and to tell the receptionist I had been bad for over two days. I got an appointment at the end of the day. A neighbour gave us a lift, the doctor looked at me, touched my stomach and picked up the phone in some alarm. My appendix had already burst and I was been poisoned from within. He wanted an ambulance but Dad's wife decided I should return home, collect an overnight bag and we would get a lift with the neighbour. She never grasped how seriously ill I was becoming. That night I had emergency surgery for appendicitis. I was in hospital for a week.

Life wasn't easy for me but I am sure compared to my sister's life, it was easy. Dad liked his beer and nights were spent in the local pub watching them both drink. Fridays and Saturdays were the worst; it was always the same thing, them getting drunk, Dad splashing the cash on his wife and me sat watching. It wasn't so much terrible as it was boring. I had nice things bought for me to compensate and I felt guilty for the fact that I got more than my sister. It was almost like favouritism and I didn't like it because it caused friction. My sister started to visit less and less, even though she was only three miles away in the next village.

Mum finally had the strength to leave her second

husband, though she had a tough time doing so. I tried to help if I stayed over. I would meet my sister and pick up my stepbrother from school. The house was a better place without him but financially it was very tough for them. It wouldn't have hurt for my Dad to lend a hand and support my sister, but he looked at it differently, he was bringing up me and it was my Mum's responsibility to bring up my sister. I felt it was quite selfish and caused even more friction between us all.

My Dad's wife was getting more unbearable and the rules were getting more tedious by the day. I wasn't being allowed to grow up and I was dressed in unfashionable clothing. The other kids picked up on it and were giving me a hard time. I wish she could have had a child of her own then I would be out of the limelight, but medically she couldn't.

My secondary school was no better than all my primary schools. I found it hard to mix and socialise. I don't know whether it was a product of all the changes of school or the shifting from home to home. All I knew was I still had a thing inside which wanted me to run and be alone. When I was alone I felt safe.

I had my first experience of a family death at the age of 11 years. I came home from school and Dad was at home, this was strange as he never was home until after 6pm. He looked stressed and I just thought it was a bad day at the office. I was sat down at the dinner table and he told me Granddad had died. I didn't know how to feel and he didn't show any emotion when he told me. Was this the manly way of dealing with death?

That night we picked up my sister and went to my auntie's. Grandma was there but the only person who showed any emotion was my auntie. The night was spent playing computer games with my cousins. I chatted with my sister and we felt we wanted to go to the funeral. This caused an argument on a grand scale. My Dad's wife decided she knew best and it wasn't a place for us. I got angry and shouted back, he was my Granddad. I should decide if I went or not, not her. In the end, we were allowed to go.

The funeral was a week later at the crematorium, no church service as my Granddad's opinion on church was always telling the vicar, "When he came to watch him work during the week, he would go on a Sunday."

I was sat in the second row with my sister, Dad's wife and uncle. Up front were my Grandma, Great auntie, Dad and auntie. Watching the coffin been wheeled in it was strange to think of him being in it. I don't know why I wanted to go so much, was it a morbid fascination? When they mentioned his name I burst into tears, this set other people off. My Dad just sat emotionless; was he that strong? When we left the service Dad had taken himself away, when he returned his eyes were bloodshot but I didn't see any tears.

Over the next few months the old routine returned. I followed my Dad and his wife to the pub to watch them get drunk, interspersed with a few nights spent at my Mum's house with my sister and stepbrother. The weekends were again spent watching Dad get drunk. Things at school were not getting any easier; I longed to fit in, but I just didn't. Groups I latched onto wanted me around as a source of amusement, someone to ridicule and beat up on. My family didn't have a clue but I refused to show any more signs of weakness.

I found solitude in the woods and wide open spaces away from the world. I'd stay here for hours until the last possible second. I had to be in by 5pm even at this age. I would sprint back, pushing myself hard until my lungs wanted to burst, I was strong.

One day I timed my run wrong, I was late and filthy

from my day's adventures in the woods. I was only a few minutes late but when I got home I knew I was in for it. I had never been physically abused by Dad's wife, just verbally punished. I feared my Dad though and I thought he was the strong man. I don't think physically he had a drinker's physique, but he talked big when dealing with obtuse people, he took no shit from waiters or anyone, if things were bad he barked, his bark scared me senseless. The verbal abuse this time came from his wife and I felt the rage inside me again. I hadn't felt this amount of rage for a few years, something snapped, I answered her back, I had done it in the past but not in this way. I was shaking, it was here again, hate, why was she saying these things? I shouted back at her, then it came, the physical, she had to put the balance back onto her side. I was thrown on the stairs, she threatened to throw me in a bath as I was filthy. I told her she couldn't. Well, that was like showing a red rag to an already raging bull. A bath was run and I was thrown in it fully clothed, mocked and had photos taken off me.

Clean clothes were thrown into the bathroom. I was raging, I was upset, she couldn't see this, the tears flowed, not sadness but anger, tears like this flowed from me often.

"Bitch," I had to run, I locked the door and planned my escape, fresh clothes and all. I opened the bathroom window and jumped across the gap to a neighbour's wall.

"Don't look down its only one floor," I said to myself.

Shaking I jumped, next skirting around the wall, keeping low and out of sight. I made it I was free, right now what? Grandma's house? Mum's house?

No, it was time I just left and got away, just get away that was the answer. Even though everyone I knew lived within a five mile radius, I didn't want them, they would make me go back and I feared what would come next from my Dad. It was winter so it was dark and cold, I made a bee-line for the woods.

It was spooky but I remembered what an uncle had told me, "If you ever need to run away, go somewhere quiet. Don't head to a town or populated place, get to the country and no one will find or hurt you."

I wasn't prepared, no jacket or money but it didn't matter, so what if it was cold or I got hungry. I found shelter in a blown down tree and I just wrapped myself in a hollow. I hated her nearly as much as I hated others from my past all those who had hurt my Mum and my family.

What seem like hours passed. I was thirsty so I went to the stream and drank from it. It was turning icy cold, so I decided to go for a walk about. I didn't think where, I just trudged around the area. I knew all the paths and places as I found solitude there in daylight, but at night it was a different place. Bats, shadows, night animals, all the noises amplified in my head and I felt as someone was watching me from behind every tree. I ended walking into the park where there were some of the people from my year at school. They were surprised to see me, no jacket, dirty, shivering, but above all, out after five o'clock.

I told them I had run off and not to let anyone know they had seen me, then I saw car brake lights slam on, then reversing lights.

"Shit!" It was my dad.

I jumped a wall and hid, he bellowed at the other kids, but they just hurled abuse back, when he realised I wasn't there, he sped off, wheels spinning. They realised I couldn't go back not to that, a few had some money and gave it me so I could get some food from the shop. One even gave me a jumper.

Then it started, they were bored with compassion, the mocking started. First calling me a liar and saying I would be back at school the next day. I handed back the jumper and the money, except one of them wouldn't take it. I thanked him and headed back to the woods before my Dad returned for a second look. I'd been away hours and I was hungry, I knew the area was being scouted but I decided to make a break for a local off licence. I thought I would be safe in a neighbouring village some four miles away.

I just got some food, when it was all over for me, I was walking down the street. A squeal of tyres, I didn't have to turn around, I knew it was him, my Dad had caught up with me. It was pointless trying to outrun a car, time for some quick thinking. He yelled for me to get in the car; people were twitching the curtains. If I had been on top of my game, I would have run and maybe someone would have called the police. I was scared though and just got in the car to be greeted with a cuff around the head and a verbal tongue lashing. I was in for it when we got in; I was to be sent away to boarding school. This sent my brain spinning, boarding school, no more of this place, no more of her.

I had been gone several hours, he couldn't break down the bathroom door as I had locked it and they hadn't been able to use the bathroom. We got back and the verbal onslaught continued. I was ordered to climb up the wall, jump the gap and open the bathroom door from the inside. As I opened it, I got another cuff from her as she shoulder charged me out so she could get to the loo.

That night I just maintained I couldn't remember what had set me off when I was questioned about why I had run. Throughout it all it became apparent it wasn't my safety they were concerned about, it was about them. I just stuck it out not budging from my story. The next day I returned to school, my Dad dropping me off at the door. This is what it was going to be like, I was grounded for three months, his threat of boarding school never mentioned again. The kids from the night before mocked me and ridiculed me. I just withdrew further, things churning away in the background. When school was finished I was picked up. When I got home I found the windows had been screwed shut. They said, "Let's see you break out now!" Did they think this could stop me?

I can't remember when it first actually happened, whether I was 11 or 12 years? All I know is what happened next was to change my life even further. It the weekend, the usual was happening. I was staying in while my Dad and wife, were going out for a meal, tonight it was with my Dad's best friend, my godfather. I always called him uncle and his children were my cousins.

His son, my Dad's godson, who was two or three years older, was going to be looking after me. I was upstairs watching television wrapped in my duvet as the house was freezing. He was upstairs with me.

I had never had the birds and the bees talk, I didn't need it. I found out by myself, mainly from my Dad's collection of pornographic literature hidden under the stairs.

It was during a TV programme that he asked if I had kissed anyone or done anything with girls or seen anyone naked. I confessed to my Dad's collection of porn and he wanted to see, so I got a few magazines and gave them to him. As he read I looked at the pictures for a minute, but turned my attention back to the TV.

It was then he did it. He took out his erect penis and started to masturbate right next to me on my bed. I didn't know what to do. I tried to watch TV but he started to encourage me to watch him. He was a strong character and a big swimmer so there was no way I could take him on. So I watched and this got him more excited. I started to feel aroused, was it wrong?

Inside it felt wrong, even sick, I was still under the duvet;

fully clothed, confused about why my body had reacted like it did. I saw my first male ejaculation, not by me, but someone I called a cousin, he wiped himself, smiled and went downstairs. I was confused; I put my Dad's magazines back and went downstairs. I asked what had just happened and asked if I was gay or was he? I was told no to both, but next time we could try a few things to experiment if I wanted. I didn't want to but I was told it was OK, it was normal. I went to bed that night with images of him playing with himself, I had a sick feeling; my head kept asking the same question, what was wrong with me? Was this my fault?

It was to happen every four weeks religiously, they all went out for a Saturday meal and my cousin would mind me. He always would find a way to be next to me and to masturbate. The more it happened, the more I though it was natural, and I started to ignore the fact I got aroused as he did it. He encouraged me to do it to myself, but I refused until one night he wanted to play a game called Dare.

It started out with silly things like pinching a swig out of one of the spirit bottles or something similar. Then it was physical challenges, I enjoyed sport but wasn't encouraged to follow anything, with Dad it was always the academic route I had to follow. So I had to do 100 push-ups or masturbate. This was after a couple of swigs of some spirit or other. Of course I failed, a dare was a dare. He went and got me a porno magazine and, embarrassed, I took out my penis and began to do what I had seen him do many times before.

The combination of the booze and encouragement meant I was OK with him watching or, at least I thought it was OK. It didn't take long until I came in front of him so I dared him right back. He didn't even attempt the push ups; he just got his erection out and played.

It then escalated, it was always the dare of 100 push-ups or masturbate. I always tried but never could manage them all.

Things had moved on to touching each other, him on me and me on him. After around six months, it moved up to the next level, to oral sex. I was constantly reassured it was natural and that we weren't gay. It only ever happened the once because after the first time he did it to me, I felt rage, it had returned. I knew this was wrong but school was constantly tormenting me, I hated being at home around Dad's wife, I was really unhappy but he made me feel like I was special.

I came to realise though that I had never suggested anything, I was brought on slowly, even manipulated, I hated it. I wasn't experimenting as I never wanted him to show me or touch me. I was too weak to fight, a mistake that will never be made in the future.

Fate took its course. I had been practising my push-ups and finally hit the magic 100. It wouldn't happen again, but something bigger happened. I was visiting my Mum; she had a new boyfriend who visited most weekends and she seemed to be finally happy.

My Dad phoned up and said we were to meet him outside, we sat in the back of the car my sister and I, he turned to face us and said he had something to tell us. He was unwell, since childhood he had suffered from a blood pressure related illness, he now had renal failure. I looked at my sister, what was that?

He explained his kidneys had failed and he needed dialysis 3 times a week but his employer supported him and he would continue working. My sister ran out of the car crying. I just sat as it was no big deal to me. Dad asked me if I understood and I told him I did and then he asked me to go after my sister and be there for her.

That's what stopped the Dare game. Dad stopped going out, so I didn't see my cousin alone, when we did it was at family functions. I didn't know one abuse had stopped but another was about to begin

# CHAPTER EIGHT

# WEIGHING IN

When I think back all I remember are the bad times, they always fill my head. I am sure at some point I had some good times, I just can't remember them. After all it only takes one bad time to make you forget one hundred good times.

Dad announcing his illness didn't really affect me. Things ticked by; his wife was still annoying me and with the annoyance came a new sense of anger from her. I keep trying to remember why it happened. Was it me who caused it? I wasn't sure. I always seemed to be in the wrong place, so maybe I brought all of these things on myself?

It all changed when the company my Dad worked for made an excuse and once again he was made redundant. With him visiting hospital three times a week, finding employment was now impossible and he stopped looking. This seemed to fuel his illness; maybe compounded by the boredom and monotony of being at home 24/7.

The arguments increased between myself and my Dad's wife, always about little things. I was growing up, she still insisted on treating me like a six year old child so I naturally pushed back. On one occasion I pushed back, not physically, just verbally and I got a good cuff from her. It was never in front of my Dad though. It always took place in the kitchen or upstairs and then the argument would rage from me because she had hit me. This sent my Dad into a rage as all he could hear was us two shouting at each other.

I'm sure this didn't help his illness, nor did the lack of money coming into the house after he'd been made redundant. I had to take my anger and channel it, she made me so mad, I wanted to lash out but I had control. A few years earlier, I had been bought a racing bike and now despite being told I couldn't, I found myself riding further and further.

I ignored curfew times not caring what the consequence would be when I returned. School had changed again, but this time to the high school where you studied right through till you were 18, if you chose to stay and do A-levels. Even changing schools yet again didn't help me fit in. I was always the weak kid, I regarded myself as being out of shape, was it the sexual abuse or the fact I let a woman beat me at home?

Whichever it was, I decided to enrol in the local gym. At the time no one really worked out, after all it was the late 80s and it still had a bit of a stigma. It was here that I found I finally fitted in somewhere.

The owner was a real fine guy who took me under his wing, instructed me on correct technique, and set me weight training programmes. I loved it as nobody teased me or tormented me. I felt a part of it and it helped calm my anger. If I wasn't made angry by my home life or school, all I did was close my eyes and remember my cousin. These thoughts made my anger worse. I had to be strong, there was no room for any more weakness. My weights were increasing and I could push through any pain barrier and complete rep after rep, set after set.

I was constantly told by the gym owner I was overdoing it but I finally felt good about something and I was going every day after school. Soon he became aware it wasn't about the training, it was about not going home. I started to look for other things outside school, again so I didn't have to go home. I still had my bike and loved to ride, but I needed something else, so I joined the Air Cadets. Again here I fitted in, I don't know whether it was the fact in some way we all were misfits, even geeks, but we all got on. There was no overt bullying. Admittedly there was the discipline of your uniform and the drill, but it also led to firing weapons, camps and friendship.

It was here I met someone who became my best friend, he was a year older, but we shared the same passion for cycling and soon I had someone I could rely on. Finally I found someone I could really call friend. Little did we know, 22 years later, we would still be the best of friends. He is the person who never judged, who understood, who helped me through some dark days and when he needed me I was always there. It was more than friendship he was family.

Even though I tried to stay out of the house, when I was there things were no easier. I would take the flack. Some days when it got too much I would just decide to go and walk over to see my Mum or Grandma. Sometimes I just found the solitude of the woods; anything not to be in the same house as her. Now I had the strength to walk out, I started to get in with the wrong sort of people at school. They had picked up on my anger and I was becoming strong from the gym. I had an attitude of not caring, I started setting bins alight, damaging cars, tormenting younger people. I was going off the rails.

The only time I felt normal was in the gym or at Air Cadets. I was turning into a nasty angry person and I hated myself for it. I had to find another outlet, another reason to stay away from home and use this anger. I found it in martial arts.

I enrolled in a notoriously hard academy and learned the art of semi- and full-contact sport karate and kick boxing. Although this taught me more discipline, it also taught me how to fight. No longer were they going to hurt me. I drifted away from the wrong sort of people and found I had a great discipline inside. I found at last I could control my anger and only unleash when I had to. I had already learned very quickly through the bullying from school and my home life how to take a punch. My discipline from Cadets and martial arts, combined with the strength from the weights, led to one thing, me turning out to be pretty decent at sport. Not team sports though as I couldn't rely on anyone else.

My new interests were never recognised at home, nothing was. I took myself off to my clubs and new hobbies, either by bus or by bike. It didn't matter if it was a 15 mile ride either way. I also funded them myself and I kept in control of them not the other way round. I had been doing jobs for years, milk rounds, paper rounds, but then I landed the peach of all jobs for a 13 year old, working in a concrete lintel factory. They loved my ability to lift concrete steps, pull steel bars, fill mixers and even drive forklift trucks. It would never happen now with health and safety, but it was a great place to work.

The owner was a hard arse, who barked orders and had temper tantrums. The only regular workers had even been known to get a clip around the ear, but he did look after his boys and it helped increase my strength and discipline.

I still didn't fit in at school but less people picked on me. The few that did where trying to prove something, to who I don't know. I took whatever they could throw at me but it was brewing, there was an explosion on the horizon. I was going to boil over, with the pressure from school and from home. Dad was the same, his wife was angry and I argued back. Now when the punches rained, with my martial arts skills, I could duck, weave and block but with blocking it looked like I was hitting back and not just knocking her hands away.

One day her Mum and Dad were visiting and they witnessed an argument and me blocking the punches, so now it was three of them against me. I assessed with my new skill I could work out a punch and kick combination which would disable all of them. Inside I told myself not to, I wouldn't let myself or my martial arts down. I wouldn't hurt these people and lose control.

My Dad shouted for it to stop. It didn't though and this time it had gone too far both for him and me. I needed out. They all conceded and had returned to the living room. I packed a kit bag and headed off to Mum's or Grandma's, anywhere but this hell hole.

Mum had settled with her new man, a fine guy who she married, but that led to a jealous household. My sister who for years had stood by my Mum through all the hard times was now not getting the same amount of attention, and she hated it. My Mum's new husband had three children of his own, but they lived 100 plus miles away, so he developed a strong relationship with my younger stepbrother. I think it was because he was still saveable and had a chance of some form of stability and normality in his childhood. My sister was going off the rails just like me.

While I was staying with them after the latest family bust up a group of us including my sister would bunk off school. That led to pinching milk, breaking back into the house when everyone had gone to work and just running amuck. We got greedy instead of keeping it to a day here or there we took a full week off and tried to forge letters. It didn't work, arguments happened and it ended up with me back at my Dad's house.

So my teenage years were a real mixed bag. I had gained

discipline from my clubs and strength from my sport but I jumped from one home to another, depending on where the arguments raged the least. What didn't change was the anger inside or the need to run. I longed to fit in so I did the things which I thought would make people like me. Like stealing booze, porno mags and even growing my hair long to try and be with the rockers at school.

I had several different personalities and depending where I was depended on what was on show. One day though it happened; I finally flipped.

Sadly the gym had to close for financial reasons, but I didn't want to stop my weights, so I bought my own equipment with the money I earned from my jobs. Grandma had given me her garage as she didn't have a car any more and I made a gym, complete with punch bag, speed ball and weights. I spent hours there, it was mine and I loved it, I was away from everyone. I had returned home for dinner and was drying the dishes while my Dad's wife washed them. An argument about something minor started but I chose to take the moral high ground and ignore the bitch. She then punched me in the face and I felt blood run down my face. Her diamond ring had caught me near the eye and now I was marked. This is what turned me and I hated myself for what I did next.

The rage inside which I had being suppressing for years flew out of me, she was about to learn fear. She was about to learn how strong I was. I punched her and it only took one shot, she was hurt. I wanted to kill her, so she got it again, she screamed and screamed. I unleashed and started to choke her.

"Fuck it the bitch must die," the rage inside was telling me.

I'd had enough but fortunately for me and her, my Dad burst in the kitchen shouting, raging, demanding to know what was going on. I looked at him and stopped going at the bitch.

She screamed at him, "Get him, your son's attacking me!"

So he drew all his strength and punched me. With that punch the balance of power between me and my Dad shifted. With that one punch, I laughed at him and could see the hurt this caused in his eyes. I asked him if that's all he had got, he hit me again. I laughed louder.

"Come on old man, give it your best because this is the last time."

With that he put his hands to one side, his wife still in hysterics screaming at him. He slapped her and told her to get in the living room. She was shocked he had never done that before. Now we stood and stared at each other. We both knew who was the stronger.

I didn't give him the chance to throw me out. I went upstairs got my school bag and left. I knew it was time to leave for the last time. I slammed the door shut behind me.

What next? Where next?

For once I didn't have to rush out, no longer was someone going to search for me. I was nearly 16 but too much stuff had just happened. I set off for the place I knew I would be safe, despite the darkness, the bats and the noises which amplify and play with your head; I went back to the woods. I searched for a spot, a spot where no one could find me. When I got there the floodgates opened. With no one around, I took the opportunity to vent my weakness. I cried my heart out. Despite everything, I had just destroyed the guy I feared and respected the most and what was left of our relationship.

The next day, I went to school. I was in a bad way. Angry and unclean as the only clothes I had were what I stood up in. My face wasn't pleasant but I passed it off to people as a lucky shot at last night's kick boxing class. After all, these people didn't care about me. Then at lunch hour I was walking in the hall, I spotted a coke can. I don't know why, but sorry I do know why, I was fucked off, I kicked it into a group of girls showering them with coke and bouncing the can off one of their heads. Cheers and laughter rang out, for a nanosecond, as quickly as it started the hall fell deadly silent, I didn't know the head master was standing right behind me.

"Get to my office."

I stood outside the headmaster's office, with three thoughts around inside my head. Do I run? Do I tell the truth? Or do I play the hard arse and tell him to go fuck himself?

When I stood in front of him, he was already writing the letter to my Dad about me being expelled. I couldn't destroy him any more, yesterday was bad, we already had a big wall between us. Being expelled from school would definitely mean no going back. So I blurted it all out, the last few years of Dad's illness, the fact I didn't have school meals because we couldn't afford them. That I couldn't take welfare as I was already been picked on, and then the fights and the constant arguments.

The headmaster was stunned, he didn't know what to do, so he sent me out to his secretary's office. She showed more compassion and I had a moment of weakness, allowing the tears to roll down my cheeks. Nothing mattered any more.

It wasn't just the coke can incident. I was feeling guilty that I may have caused my Dad's illness to get worse. Was it my fault he was ill? His wife made me feel like it was and I now believed it. In the background, behind the office door, a phone call was being made to social services about a teenager at risk.

Then it all started to happen fast with a meeting with the head of a department, but not in my year. She briefed me about a social worker I was about to meet. All afternoon I was worried about the social services, would they believe me or would I be branded a liar?

The time had come, the social worker had arrived, his probing questions started as soon as I sat down. Did I let him in or just let him see some of the parts of my past? I decided I wasn't ready to let him in, so I gave him enough to put the wheels in motion. I didn't trust this guy, why should I? After the meeting, which seemed more of an interview or interrogation, he went off to talk to my Dad and his wife. I didn't fancy his prospects and I knew what was going to happen. It would be all my fault and I would be portrayed as a trouble maker. She would manipulate the situation so I would be the problem.

I decided to go off to my garage, to my gym, and do what I did best, push my body to the limit. Even then, if I didn't puke or bleed, I wasn't training hard enough. I could push through the pain, all I needed to do was think of the past, the hurt, the anger, the rage. Now I also had something new I could call on, guilt. They all drove me, I could switch off and hurt myself.

When I eventually left the gym, I felt strong. I knew I could hurt myself any time I wanted and that pain was my friend. I headed for my Grandma's to have dinner and then to my Mum's to sleep, it was when I got there the social worker turned up.

I was ready for him though as nothing could hurt me and I was strong again. I asked him, what had they said and, as I thought, was told they were shocked and I was blamed. I asked how my Dad acted and it was clear he was in denial as he said we didn't need outside help and I was blowing it out of all proportion. The social services worker then asked my Mum if could I stay with her as I had my GCSE's coming up soon and I needed a safe environment.

She said that of course I could stay. This house had its arguments too and I was thankful she didn't mention that. I wondered if I was the common link to all the arguments and pain. I knew I didn't want to stay there though as I would have to share a bedroom with my younger stepbrother. I was never asked what I wanted.

I wanted out, I didn't want any of them, I wanted to be taken away and to start a new life. I felt guilty about all these feelings of running away. Perhaps I was just thinking about me and not the other people around me. So I did what I always did, told them what they wanted to hear. I was happy to stay there and I would check in through school. Even though it was hurting me, it was my way of keeping others happy. It didn't matter I was sad.

# Chapter Nine

# The Kiss

Soon my GCSE's were over and decisions about my life were now needed.

Inside I wanted to break away, from Yorkshire, from my family. I was back living at my Dad's. It was back to normal, although there had been a power shift between us. They were trying to regain the balance to their side of the scales. I didn't want to keep troubling them, so I just left them to do whatever they needed to be happy. I didn't care anymore.

Results day came and I insisted on going alone. My Dad and his wife were overpowering, so results driven, threats, promises, but never praise with it. They'd already planned my future. I would re-sit or take A-levels. It was never about me or my sports. I ended up with 1 B grade, 7 C grades and a D, not a bad count considering. They took no time in reminding me that I could have done better.

With the results came a shift of power back to their side, and it was decided for me that I would attend higher education. I didn't want to, I just wanted out of the place but I wanted to keep the peace. I couldn't live with any more guilt and I was tired of the arguments. I tried to chat with my Dad about what I wanted from life and my desire to join the military.

Even with my experience with Air Cadets, it wasn't

the RAF I truly wanted to join. I wanted something more physical, something where I could push my limits. When I mentioned the Para's or the Marines, the answer came back "Why do you want to be cannon fodder, you need to do more than that!"

So with all my choices and decisions made for me. I was to study Economics, A/S Physics and A/S Math. Obviously I was less than enthused about the prospect of that timetable. I did manage to chat with the sports master though and I arranged to help teach PE in my free lessons.

At the end of a long summer of working at building sites, I had an opportunity to help my Dad out and build a path and a patio using waste materials from the site. At least this should get my Dad's wife off my back for a while or so I thought. Dad's health was getting worse, he was losing weight and getting weaker. The new treatment, designed to give him more freedom and take him away from the dialysis machine, was having side effects. After a tiring day of building, she did something which makes me sick thinking about it.

I was lying on my bed watching some junk on TV when she came into my room and lay on the bed next to me. Then the weirdest thing happened, she then leaned over and tried to kiss me. Trust me it wasn't me misreading anything it was an attempt at a full kiss, I turned my head and went a little red. She stood up and laughed at me walking out of my room. It was bubbling inside; I could feel the rage, for two reasons.

First she had just tried it on with me and secondly that she only did it to mock me and to test me to see what I would do. I got into my cycling gear as I knew what had to be done; I needed my garage, my punch bag I needed to hit something quick.

On the way there I was raging and pushing my bike,

that's when I lost the front end, hit the deck and it hurt. With the pain came a smile though, I was back. I was bleeding from a leg injury when I finally got to my garage, it didn't matter because that was the mildest pain I would feel tonight. I didn't use wraps for my wrists or feet, it was my punch bag's turn. I got stuck in, every punch was at her, I saw her face, her lips and heard her mocking laughter, bang, hit it again and again. I came round with a knock on my garage door it was my best friend.

When he walked in, he told me to stop hitting the bag but I just continued. He shouted at me to stop and take a look at myself. I stopped and looked in the mirror. I had blood splattered across my face but I was bemused as to where it had come from? Then I looked down and saw my knuckles were dripping red. My bag had absorbed a lot of the blood but it had started to splatter back at me, hence I was covered, What with the blood on my leg I must have looked quite a sight.

I just smiled and laughed "I feel better now!"

I cleaned up the best I could, and we headed over to the cinema for the midnight showing. The pain was still stinging my hands and leg, but with it, I felt good.

I had started back at school, the sixth form college was tagged onto my old high school and the timetable I had was horrible. The only thing I looked forward to during the week was my PE session. I was heading back to the common room when I bumped into the old head of my year; he seemed to be a good guy. We stopped for a chat, he wanted to know how things were getting on. He was pleased with my GCSE results and then he told me something which made me both angry and sad. He told me he had written to all the examination boards on my behalf, explaining my situation and the pressures of my home life and he hoped I didn't mind. My head was spinning with what he had just said and what he'd done.

I could feel it inside starting again, the rage. I thought the results I achieved were down to me and something I could finally be proud of. Had I deserved them or was it a sympathy thing? Was I a failure?

I smiled and told him I didn't mind and even thanked him for his concern but that I was now doing OK. I just wanted away from the conversation, I needed to be away. A group of so-called friends then bumped into me and they could see something in my eyes. So instead of letting me go, they fuelled me even more. They knew about my martial arts and how gym strong I was but no one had seen me blow, they chanted things, stupid things.

"Psycho, psycho."

This enraged me more, I was out of control. My first victim who was in my year had pissed me off earlier in the day. He was sitting down and I just shin kicked him with the heel of my boot. He just looked shocked, as he lifted his trouser leg, there was a perfect imprint of my boot heel. It was almost a branding and I just laughed at him. The blood then started to pour out of it, all the edges were seeping with blood.

The next victim was perched on a wall so I pulled him backwards and he took a tumble into the concrete. I just wanted to dole out the hurt but, lucky for him and me, the bell rang and it brought me back. I was due in PE so I left the tormentors and headed for the gym. I was teaching the year below me and some of them thought they were tough guys from their martial arts training and always gave me lip, but today was going to be different.

We were just getting changed, when one of them was giving me a load of mouth, we had a stand off, both in our different martial arts stances. Usually I would have walked away but not today. I hit him with a spinning axe kick, a movie shot. I hit him plum, a textbook straight over his defence and down his cheek bone. I had never used my training outside the gym so I did use a degree of self control so I didn't do him too much damage. It did stun and hurt him though.

I came around; what had I just done? The last hour I had been out of control almost like a darkness had seeped into my head and now I had broken my own martial arts discipline. I didn't bother with the lesson, I just got changed and walked out of the college. I knew where I had to go, straight to my comfort zone, my garage, my gym. Once there I knew what had to be done. It was time to teach myself self discipline again, the more it would hurt, the more discipline I would learn.

I returned to the college the next day and the group of so called tough guy martial artists came up and congratulated me on my kicking display from the day before. It was from then onwards that people began to finally leave me alone. The rumours soon went around about how I could hold my own and take it on. Later that day a challenge from the new school bully inevitably ensued but I had my discipline back. We stood off, he tried to punch I just ducked, blocked and walked away. When I was walking he decided to hit me from behind, it didn't bother me. I just turned looked at him, laughed and kept walking.

Other things were changing now too, girls were taking more of an interest. I had being playing around the last few years but now something was different. There were more party invites. I was no longer the guy on the outside of the group, but the one on the inside everyone invited. The parties were all the same. I controlled the idiots who either tried to crash it or had too much booze. I wasn't too bothered about drinking. I did do it now and again but I hated losing control. The parties led to me ending with some girl or other, they were just objects. I had no emotions to share or give them.

My best friend had already left for the RAF and we hooked up on his return on leave. It was always good to see an understanding face and hear his stories of the military. It just underlined the fact I wanted to join up and get away. After a while, I loathed college so much that I just stopped going. At least I'd chatted about it with my Mum and she confirmed to me I was only there to please my Dad. It was true. I was only trying to please him and with it I was hoping some of my pain would go but it didn't.

I soon ended up in a brick factory labouring in a factory complex just down the road from my Grandma's and my garage. This was good as it gave me a little confidence and I could train during lunch hours. I decided to try and chat things through with my Dad, to make him understand, but he wasn't happy. No college, no home, so once again I found myself living at my Mum's place.

I talked about joining the Para's and the Marines with him again. I needed him on my side, he was the only one who could sign my papers to join the military because I was still under 18, but now the usual cannon fodder remark was tagged with "What will I do if you go away for months?"

More guilt, great! If I waited until I was 18 it would be out of his hands, but could I wait that long?

So I went to the recruiting office and applied for the RAF. I was told there would be a wait as recruiting was very thin due to down sizing of the force. I wanted so much to be a Physical Training Instructor, but after my aptitude test and exam results, the recruiting officer said I would be wasted and offered me Ground Electronic Mechanic. He didn't know a lot about the trade but I was told I could re-train when and if I got in.

I trusted his advice and, after all, anything was better than the life I currently had. I told the recruiting officer all about my past home life and involvement with the social services. His advice was to keep it to myself and to tell no one about it again as it could jeopardise my chances. My history had to be between us two only, I was to keep quiet.

So I was marking time, waiting for my chance to escape from this life I was leading. My garage had been broken into and my gym was cleaned out, but I still managed, buying new equipment and setting up again a few miles away.

My Dad had come around a little and realised I wouldn't be taking any further part in education. He agreed if I joined the RAF, he would sign the papers as I wasn't going to be cannon fodder. He was that narrow minded about the military. If only he knew then I would be targeted by something worse than any cannon, he might have taken a different view.

One of the nights I was at my Dad's house for dinner, my sister arrived unexpectedly. She was clearly upset and tearful saying that my Mum's husband had hit her. This was now up to me to sort out and even my Dad told me to go and deal with the problem, as he was too ill. To be honest, if he hadn't have been ill he would have found a different excuse. He irked me up, saying I had to go and defend her. So I ran the few miles there, complete with a metal bar and with just one intention, to hurt him like he had hurt my sister.

When I got there, I just started mouthing off. I was shaking. I could feel the rage but I wouldn't let it go. Thankfully a voice inside told me I had to keep my discipline. I didn't want to feel like I had done previously and use my skills to do harm outside of the ring. We argued and I threatened him with the iron bar, but in the end I put it down. I didn't need it as I was fighting at such a high level I knew my fist and feet could do the same amount of damage. I still had the internal voice, I refused to lose discipline for anyone but I struck him just the once. It was enough to show that I cared enough about my sister and not to mess me about because I wasn't scared of anyone.

As a result, I was instantly booted out of Mum's house with my kit thrown at me. I was homeless again.

Oh well, I thought. Out of the frying pan, back into the fire. Back to my Dad and his wife. Oh joy.

The months dragged by and I kept hassling the recruiting office, constantly asking for a date of enlistment but none came. I had no contact with my Mum and my sister was living at a place in Huddersfield with her boyfriend. Everyone had rallied around to help them set up home, but it didn't last, she was soon back at my Mum's. She always seemed to pick up the wrong bloke, the ones that mistreated her verbally and physically. Some were just out and out gits. She always knew I was there if they ever got too bad.

The call came around January, the one I had been waiting for, the escape from it all. I was to be accepted into the RAF and I was to start in April, providing I passed the medical and an interview. All my references were completed by various employers and school; I was hoping no one had mentioned my past. I was to be free, away from them all, a new life, I just hoped I could break away fully though.

Inside I had my fears, not a fear of leaving but the fear of coming back. I knew someone would make me feel guilty enough so I would return. Things had eased off at home, we were tolerating each other. We were all aware the end was nearly in sight.

My Dad was trying his best to send me with the full equipment list. His income support didn't stretch far, but I appreciated everything he did for me. I was still on frosty talking terms with my Mum, I wasn't allowed to the house but I popped to her work for a tea or coffee if I was passing. Her husband wasn't ready to forgive me and I wasn't ready to say sorry. I saw it as a sign of weakness. My sister was living back home and it transpired she had elaborated the truth about my Mum's husband hitting her and some of the other boyfriend stuff. It was nothing as dramatic as I was led to believe.

April soon arrived and I was ready to go. All the goodbyes had been said. I was still only 17 years old. Various people offered to give me a lift to basic training. I was trying to please everyone and it was stressing me out, in the end, I decided I wanted to get the train, leave the station and be in my own world.

On the day I was leaving my Dad gave me a gift to help me on my way. It was a brand new Walkman as he knew I found comfort in music. I really appreciated it, more so as I knew it was his way of saying he was proud.

I accepted a lift from Dad to the railway station at Wakefield where I exchanged my military travel warrant to take me to Newark station. I hugged my Dad and even his wife too. I don't know why I hugged her, maybe for my Dad's sake or just to show I was growing up - at last. I got on the train, relief spread, a tear trickled, I now had a future and it was up to me. I had to be strong, never show weakness, even if it meant conflict, I had to prove to myself I wasn't weak. I could leave and make something for myself, I could leave my past behind. The train pulled away from the platform I waved goodbye, plugged in my Walkman. Bon Jovi's Keep the Faith played. The words rang something inside.

I settled into my seat. Looking around the carriage you could tell some of the other guys on here were going the same way as me. I kept to my Walkman as I wasn't ready to chat. Inside though I was itching to get there and start a new life.

# CHAPTER TEN

# PASSING OUT

The train journey was over before it started. Before I knew it, it was pulling into Newark station. What would happen next I wondered?

The 'what next' came in the form of a short guy in uniform, with two white stripes, I knew the rank structure from Air Cadets. He was a corporal, shouting his head off. We had not even got onto the platform before he was yelling. Many non-military people were getting off at that stop. Even they took a step backwards.

I got my kit together and headed for the short angry guy. As I approached, he took that as a cue to yell even more and louder. I'd got the idea the first time around; to get my sorry arse on the bus outside the station if I'd had joined the RAF.

I threw my kit on board and joined a throng of shell-shocked faces. It wasn't long before Mr Angry was on the bus barking at us further. I just let the seat swallow me up and tried to avoid his stare, just letting his abusive words wash over me.

Before too long, RAF Swinderby's gates loomed. The bus hadn't come to a halt before we were barked at once again. This time we were to get off the bus, we all were a shower of shit and we should line up in ranks with our bags. There was no hiding now.

I hadn't bothered with a hair cut because I already knew the barber would be the first place to visit. Even the guys who had already had the crew cut were getting another one and were made pay for it. The problem though was my hair made me stand out, so I got a face full of Mr Angry.

"Don't break, let him spit, let him get in my face, take it. This is nothing compared to the crap you've just left behind."

Soon though, all my hair had gone and I blended in. The rest of the day was form filling, issuing of kit, being placed into flights and then stuffed into 12 man billets. Basic training was to last seven weeks. There were testing times ahead as it was old school training comprising of verbal abuse, lots of PT, inspections and the odd bit of physical.

For the first few weeks, I found it hard to bond or settle with the people around me. Sleeping was a problem at first, in a room with strange people. I wasn't ever homesick but some days, I did break and I had to have a good chat from the padre. I was riddled with guilt for leaving Dad and when I did make a call home, he made sure I knew it. I kept telling him I was having a great time; I wasn't going back for anybody.

I found I could take anything they threw at me, nothing phased me, but oddly I got on with the staff more than the guys going through the same basic course as me. I also found pleasure in some of the activities which were designed to cause you discomfort, things like the respirator runs and the CS gas chamber.

Soon it was all over, the basic phase was done and I was awarded the best recruit. I don't know why, all I did was help people where I could and try my best. Some thought of it as the butt-kissing award but they were the ones who thought they were going to get it. The passing out parade was supposed to be a proud moment. My Dad, his wife and her parents all attended. I could have done without three out of the four of them being there. I did what I was getting used to, just playing the game to keep everyone happy. I did however see a flicker in my Dad's face that gave it away that, for once, he might actually be proud of me.

Boring guard duty followed keeping me at RAF Swinderby for another two weeks before heading off to RAF Locking for trade training. My heart wasn't in electronics, but in my head it was a way of not going back to my past life. I was still training hard, the gym was my release but I still found it hard to socialise. All the people around me were forced upon me. There was no private space so I found my solitude in the weights bay as most trainees had enough exercise in compulsory PT.

The RAF training was starting to get a bit fluffy for me. We weren't made to run in boots and the basic fitness test was replaced with an easier bleep running test. Peoples' attitude seemed to be that they were there to fix things and not run around. I am afraid the RAF was not what I was looking for and these trades weren't for me. It wasn't the physical testing I longed for I wanted to be elite. I knew I could push my body, and step out of my mind, to push the limits. This trade nonsense was too easy for me, not for my brain, but my body.

The sports I was involved with were not really supported by the military then. If you didn't do football or rugby, getting time off was hard. I made a stupid promise to my Dad that I wouldn't step into the boxing ring. It would have been too easy a transition but maybe given me the challenge I needed, but again I put his needs and wishes before mine. In the end, I just trained for me, but during one weight session I was asked to compete in Power Lifting. This was ideal, a way I could focus my strength and power. The only person to push me was me.

It was summer leave and I had travel warrants for two weeks off. No way was I heading back home, so I headed north to see my best mate in the north of Scotland. We had a good time but I was angry and a dark mist had started to cloud my mind when both sober and drunk. I wanted to see if I was as good as I thought I was, so I would do silly things like running back to his room from miles out. My head was in constant overdrive and if I had a beer I would explode.

One night on my adventures I went to the local park, looking for trouble and I found it in a group of lads. We were all around the same age, I was English, obviously military and outnumbered. They fancied giving someone a kicking and I was their target. It was fun, the group mentality they were all talk, we all stood off from each other. They threw the first punch. I just smiled as I blocked it and then I went for it. I took some shots but I gave out more, some went down easy but I was employing the tactics I had been taught in kickboxing. My club, despite all the martial arts rules and discipline, wanted you to be able to look after yourself on the street so we got taught how.

"If they cannot breathe, they cannot fight. If they are on the floor they cannot fight either!"

In the movies they are all elaborate kicks and combinations designed to look good on screen. It doesn't work. In the real world, nothing is choreographed, you have to think on your feet. I was outnumbered so the moves I used were ones designed to stop them in their tracks. Some ran when they knew I could fight. I had taken some good shots but was still fighting. They had helped stem my anger. It felt good, soon it was over and I was happy with the outcome. For the first time, I didn't feel guilty about using my skills.

When I returned after the summer break, I was still angry and trying to prove a point to everyone about me fighting the world. I wasn't the biggest but I never would back down. Everything was a challenge as to how I could handle things. It was a way of staying in control.

I also liked to help people out, especially those who were classed as weak. I was always trying to be a white knight to people in trouble, just so I could take the focus off my life and maybe help them.

This got me into trouble one night in the NAAFI. A few of us ended up trading insults and the odd punch was thrown. It was something and nothing, but on a training base, discipline was harsh. I had got back to my room when there was a thump on the door, I opened it to find an RAF policeman there. I was arrested and thrown in the cells for the night. I found it comforting, it was peaceful, the other guy involved was in the next cell to me. The next day we were released but a few weeks later the charge came through. It had at least been dropped from assault to just threatening behaviour. I ended with a fine and jankers (a punishment of restricted duties; parading morning and evening in immaculate uniform, working your daily job, and working extra hours doing meaningless tasks such as painting stones, shining brass radiators etc). It wasn't too bad, you just had to get your head down and get on with it, I still maintained my gym sessions in between cleaning and polishing my kit.

During one of my gym sessions, I experienced my first severe injury. During a heavy shoulder press, my shoulder locked and the weight caused my shoulder to pop. I ended up with a sling and was bounced between doctors and physios.

My first real taste of military medical care wasn't a pleasant one, I was messed around, the doctors' pain scale is so subjective, and trust me I can take pain. They couldn't find a quick fix, so I was left with the sling, finally I got an operation. The operation didn't fix the problem so I was put in rehab, but this just led to another big problem in my life. With my arm in a sling walking jarred my shoulder, and sitting on a bike jarred my shoulder. The pain was unbearable but even worse it took away the one thing which made me feel normal, which made me feel alive, my only escape, the safety of a gym.

# CHAPTER ELEVEN

# THE FIRST CUT IS THE DEEPEST

Remarkably I passed the course at RAF Locking and was soon away to my proper first posting as a Leading Aircraftsman. I'd been given the theory but I was very green to the big wide world of the military. Training systems can never prepare you for what is about to happen.

I had a nightmare first posting. It was in the one place I didn't want to go back to. The closest base to my home was 75 miles north and I was posted into it. This meant I would be expected home on a more regular basis to help sort things out.

As you might expect, I had started to do things to annoy people at home. I was told never to get a tattoo and if you do don't bother coming back. So I got one and could still go home. The goal posts were then changed to never get a motorbike, so I got one of those too.

I made some close friends within the section but not close enough to share any of my demons with. I was back to using woman as objects in a trophy cabinet, just to prove I was normal, but again I couldn't feel any emotional attachments to them. The section was full of big drinkers and I started to be one too.

My nightmares had never left, but without the gym to deal with my emotions, I was really moody and in a dark place. The last thing I needed was to drink but in some ways it gave me comfort. I was making weekly trips home to sort out my shoulder with a local osteopath; it was helping my body but not my head. Dad's illness had taken a turn for the worse and if I was in a dark place, he was in a darker one. When I was home, I tried to spend time with him, but I got constant guilt trips about finances, his illness, how life was really bad for him.

On one of his darkest days, he even talked of killing himself. This led me to thinking of what a joy it would be if he did die, how I would be free from his wife and from this place, where all the bad things had happened to me. Just going back there and sleeping in the same room were constant reminders of my past and fuelling my ever increasing dark mood. Thinking thoughts of him dying though just led to more guilt but with  no channel to send it down.

It all came to a head one day after a boozy evening in the rugby club. My drinking had got out of control. The guys around me loved it because I fitted in with their ethos but inside, terrible thoughts were about to spill out. I had an argument with a colleague, this led to me getting upset, it wasn't about the argument, it was about my home life, but they were not to know it. I took an empty bottle of beer, smashed it and cut my forearm, it was a nasty deep gash.

People stared in disbelief at what I had done, they thought it was because of the stupid argument but they didn't know, I wouldn't let them in. I was engulfed in my own dark thoughts and needed pain. My shirt was cut and now crimson with blood, the wound needed stitches, but I ignored it. When I looked down and saw what I had done, I just laughed. My shoulder was still too painful to train on, so I had found a new way to cause pain by cutting myself. I was alive again.

I looked around the rugby club and people had backed away. I don't blame them because I was a drunk, out of control crazy person, with a smashed beer bottle and blood dripping from a self cut. Only the barmaid was brave enough to come over. She had become a friend and asked why I had just done it. She took me outside and started to pry.

I told her about the guilt of my Dad's illness and him wanting to end it all. That seemed to stop her curiosity. She went back inside to fetch a guy who had also become a close friend. They brought a beer towel, I wrapped my arm in it and we set off back to the billet block. The foggy darkness started to lift. I could feel pain but now in a different way. When we got into my room, my friend decided it would be safer to remove all my sharps; razor, knives and bottles. All just so I wouldn't do anything crazy again. My arm was still dripping in blood but I still refused treatment.

"It'll be OK in the morning," I told him.

After a coffee or six and when the wound had stopped bleeding, he decided it was safe to leave me.

"I'll return first thing with your razor so you can shave before work," he said.

I sat up all night thinking of what had done, looking down at the cut and smiling, feeling the sensation of pain around my body. It felt good but the horror soon dawned. How will I explain it away to friends and family? In the end I came up with a classic bar fight story. I got hit with a bottle and put my arm in the way to defend my face.

In the morning, true to his word, my razor was returned but I was monitored. He took it back to his room then we were off to the section. The crew room was quiet as everyone knew what I had done. Thankfully nobody wanted to discuss it but, in the end, my Chief took me into his office and I had to explain myself to him. He just blamed the booze and he didn't want to know any history. This suited me as I didn't want him involved, so I promised it was an isolated incident and it wouldn't happen again.

So the next time I was home, and the scar was visible, I just explained it off as a bar fight and everyone believed me. Why wouldn't they? Only I knew the truth. That first cut reminded me of escaping the pain in my head in the same way I had been using the gym.

The prognosis on my shoulder was good and, in the next few months, I would be back to full fitness and training. I knew when that happened I could keep the darkness out but for now I had to keep fighting the darkness, especially the darkness of home. What would I do next time I needed to feed my desire for pain, my desire to escape to a better place than my head?

Eventually when my shoulder was fixed enough for me to start back training, it was sadly only light cardio work and it just didn't cut the mustard in pushing me. I had to be careful, it took the edge off the darkness a little but not to the extent I needed.

One weekend, when I was chatting with my Dad, he was in his usual dark place too. It had been made worse by the doctors telling him, due to his weakened state, his chance of receiving a transplant was minimal as he had little chance of surviving the surgery. This led to another bout of self pity which I wasn't taking any guilt for. When he talked about ending things and how life was bad, I just wanted out of it. I felt for his suffering but he was always quick to point out how I was making my life OK and I wasn't home enough and didn't care about them anymore.

I needed my fix. The bike wasn't going to give me the pain I needed so I looked at my arm and remembered the pain I felt when I cut it. How can I feel a little pain just to help? Then a light bulb came on. My first tattoo didn't hurt but it was uncomfortable enough to remind me I was still alive. So with that I went for a second tat, this time just to feel pain.

# CHAPTER TWELVE

# TRANSPLANT

Things started to settle down for the next few years. I tried to conform to what people expected. I got a regular girlfriend but I never let her in. When the word love was mentioned, I shied away from it. If I couldn't love myself, how could I love another person?

I met some guys from the Special Air Service (SAS) who were on a course out of the base. I started to train with them, running, weights, every time they were out, I was with them. It was great to find a bunch of guys who seemed to push like I did. I was told about their training and it was suggested I should try out. I was gobsmacked and flattered, but I made the mistake of telling my Dad about it. Why did I want to do it? Why did I want to be cannon fodder? Who would help him out if I was away? The same script, the same guilt, so I put it out of my brain.

I put him first again. I didn't fit in playing with radars and radios. It wasn't me, it wasn't who I wanted to be in the military. When the SAS guys described their lifestyle and training, it really appealed to me. Again I did the honourable thing and put my Dad first.

Dad's illness was getting worse, he had wasted away from 14 to 15 stone to under ten stone and with it came pain and self pity. I managed to block it out as I found a new buzz in drug-free bodybuilding. It was ideal I could train pushing my limits and no one questioned it because it was a sport.

One Monday, I was sat in the crew room at work and my Chief walked in and asked me for a word. I wondered what had I done this time. He said he had just taken a phone call from my Dad's wife and he was going for a kidney transplant that afternoon. I just looked on at him, trying to process the information. I remembered what had been said and I knew his chances of survival weren't good, so I shrugged my shoulders and looked at him and said, "Well that's a funeral I will have to go too."

My chief just looked at me in disbelief. I explained his chances and eventually I asked the practical questions like which hospital and when?

He told me it was scheduled for this afternoon in St James's Hospital, Leeds and if I wanted, I could go straight away. I just left the office headed back to the crew room for a brew and chilled out. I was thinking how relieved I was, his pain was nearly over and I could move on too, leave his wife behind and maybe, just maybe start my life over. For the first time I didn't feel guilty for feeling that way. I wanted him to find peace.

When my Chief came back into the crew room some time later, he was shocked to see me still there. He told me I should go or I would feel guilty if something happened. Secretly I wanted something to happen. I left work, packed a bag and headed south down the A1. By the time I got to St James's and found the correct ward, I just saw my Dad being wheeled into the elevator to be taken down to the operating theatre. He didn't see me and I just looked on. Dad's wife called at me, she was in tears. What was I supposed to do, comfort her? I decided I better and gave her a hug.

She then told me the call came in yesterday and they had been up all night discussing it. At that point the comforting stopped. If they couldn't be bothered to phone me then why should I bother giving her a shoulder to cry on now? I didn't want to be involved in the decision, it wasn't my place, but at least they could have warned me earlier. I could have got myself together and maybe have come to the hospital to chat with my Dad before his operation. It would have been a chance to set things straight, not just for my sake, his too.

We went our separate ways, she headed for her family close by in Leeds and I headed for my Grandma's in Huddersfield. I felt it was my duty to go and tell people, Grandma, sister, auntie and my godfather. The very least I could was keep them in the picture because nobody else was. When my duty was done, it was time to hit the gym. A new gym had been opened nearby by the same guy who had trained me years ago, using much of his old equipment. It felt like home, a friendly place with a friendly smile and a chance for me to get my head straight by my usual method.

The next day, to my surprise, Dad had survived his operation and was in recovery. Grandma wanted to visit as soon as possible so I said I would take her over. When we entered his room he looked in a bad way as he was wired up to this and that machine.

Then, to my surprise, he looked straight at me and started to have a go about something. I couldn't believe my ears, the first thing he said to me was an angry guilt-ridden exchange about something trivial. I felt it again, burning inside, I had been relieved when I was told he had survived the transplant but now I wish he hadn't.

I walked straight out of the room leaving everyone there. Sod him. On the way past my Grandma I said for her to meet me in the café, my visit was over for the day. When Grandma came down to find me she knew I was upset about what had been said. I was somewhere else at that point, she told me it was the drugs inside him. How I wished I could tell her about the problems over the years and the guilt and conversations between us, but it wasn't fair for me to do that. I had to protect her from the pain, I just agreed with her and said I understood. I didn't visit for a few days until I took my Grandma back, it was frosty but I did it for her, nobody else.

Over the next few months, Dad grew stronger as the transplant was a success although his heart was weakened by the whole ordeal. He'd had a few mild heart attacks in the past. With his new strength he started to ease up on me and was pleasant to spend time with. I had done two body building competitions and placed second in both had been invited to the British finals.

Although I invited people to join me for support, only a few made the effort. My Mum was one of them, throughout all my teenage years of sport no one had ever bothered. This time she did and it was nice to have her in the audience, although later that night she said something which started me thinking. It was about my past and how she was sorry for the disjointed childhood and how she wasn't always there for me. I just sat there and let her off-load all of her guilt in my direction. Great now I had both parents doing it in two different ways.

What do you say to it? It doesn't matter? I'm fine about it? When actually you are not fine.

I tried to do the honourable thing and said nothing except, "Don't worry about it, I'm OK."

She didn't ever mean for me to feel guilty but I did. The conversations always started with how she was feeling but it always got twisted and I then felt it was my fault and that I'd been the reckless one.

In all of this I had still managed to stay with the same girlfriend, I still hadn't let her in to my dark past and at times I had indiscretions with other girls. I didn't care if I got caught or not, the more I played away the more I was accepted by colleagues.

I had some leave and during a shopping trip with my girlfriend my phone bleeped. It was one of the first mobiles that was so big it never fitted in your pocket. It was my Chief at work, I was being posted from Leeming to Stornoway.

I hadn't requested a posting at Stornoway. This was an out of area posting. Go to North Scotland, turn left, get on a ferry for a few hours and there you have it, a little island. I was leaving in 56 days, the minimum notice the military could give you. I wasn't bothered even though I had concerns about my Dad. He seemed to being relying on me increasingly after his operation.

When I came off the phone, I turned to my girlfriend and told her, the reaction wasn't pleasant. She started to cry and people were looking on like I'd hit her she was making that much drama. Through the sobs, she asked how she could come with me. I said the only way was if we ever got married, with that the tears stopped a smile appeared. Apparently I had just proposed, before my feet touched the ground or my brain caught up with my mouth I was signing for a diamond ring and she was planning a party.

Later in the day, I broke the news to my family that I was off and they had to accept it. I explained it was my job and it was out of my hands. If only I had been clever enough earlier in my career to tell people it was work's decision and not mine, I might have found what I was looking for from the military and I wouldn't be hating what I was doing.

When I got to Stornoway, I settled in quickly. It was a small unit of 24 guys and with the small size you all had extra duties. I was to sort out peoples' fitness, the gym, and the sports kit. Perfect.

My new engagement soon fell apart as my heart was never in it, I ended it within days of arriving with one swift phone call. I was soon back to treating the opposite sex like a conquest and challenge. I just couldn't let anyone get close.

I made friends throughout the island mainly because on my free days and evenings I helped out the local council gym instructing people. I felt free there I didn't have to think about the past. My darkness appeared to have gone, there were no reminders, the only time to revisit the past was when I chose to phone home, which I did infrequently.

On the airfield, there was a civilian helicopter search and rescue unit. I was interested in what they did and managed to get on a flight. The winchman's job looked like a challenge so I decided it was for me and asked how to apply.

They suggested re-training and doing it from within the RAF. Coming from a fast jet unit I didn't appreciate the helicopter aspect of the RAF. Soon I was studying and training for the selection process. Physically I was fine, but in my head, I had to be elite. So I set about running around the island in rig, boots and a heavy bergan (military issue rucksack), along with a punishing gym regime. I was to become very fit.

I studied for 18 months before even applying and when I did, I didn't tell anyone back home. I didn't want them to put me off my decision. This time it was for me.

The base at Stornoway was to be closed, it belonged to Nato and they were no longer going to fund it so we were going to be the last military men there. We were then all moved to Kinloss, north of Inverness.

My selection interviews started early 1998 and I was progressing well. Before I knew it, I had dates for a four-day selection programme at RAFC Cranwell.

The mental challenge was interesting and candidates were asked to leave at different points because they didn't cut the mustard. I managed the full four days and at the end you were sent back to your unit and informed later of the decision.

I was marking time, wondering what was to happen next, then the message was filtered down from boss to boss. I had passed and had been selected to start retraining as Airman Aircrew as an Air Load Master. The only downside to this was heading south again, this time to Lincolnshire and back near my family and my past.

This time I had changed, I was stronger. The time away from them had seen to that, the darkness had gone, for now at least.

# CHAPTER THIRTEEN

# SURVIVAL OF THE FITTEST

It was back to basic training, having already gone through the RAF Swinderby regime. Having watched the force change over the last six years, I knew it wouldn't be as tough, I was wrong. Having to go back to basics is a test of character, it's a game, you play by their rules, at their pace. The most frustrating thing was I was losing fitness.

It was hard to live in a room with all these different personalities and not clash. So I made sure I stayed away from home while I was there so I didn't tip the balance back towards the dark. I managed to keep it together for the sixteen weeks, the end of the course arrived and I finally passed out as an acting Sergeant.

It was a proud day, a day I decided to share with both Dad and Mum and their partners in the Sergeants' Mess.

Being an ex-ranker going into the Sergeants' Mess meant a great deal to me, it was like hallowed ground, but the day was soon diluted, they brought the past back, my frustration and anger grew by the second after I overheard a conversation.

The usual happened the training staff felt duty bound to tour the guests and they always shared a story about the course. Then it was the guests turn, I heard my Dad and his wife talking about my childhood, how proud they were and how I was no trouble growing up and what a joy I had been. Were they talking about the same person?

I looked around. Surely they couldn't be talking about me? It was surreal to hear it, especially from her. I was no bother growing up? Why did they have to mention my past? Why couldn't they skirt the issue? Why was I in earshot when they said it? Was it a reminder? Or was it their way of blocking it out and pretending the bad stuff never happened?

Thankfully my Mum and husband just enjoyed the day, nothing about our past was mentioned and I was glad.

The next day I was still thinking about what had been said. Still hungover and angry, I reached for my runners, I knew a place where I could run, a short hill where we did sprint reps, that was for me today. I got there, not feeling great, I had to bury my past back in my head.

I had to be stronger than the darkness and bury it deep inside. Sprint to the top, jog back down, repeat. I kept doing it and doing it until eventually my body let go, I was sick, a combination of the physical and the hangover. It felt good, nice to be back in control. I jogged back to my new home, the Sergeants' Mess, to get myself cleaned up and prepare for my next posting as the next part of training was delayed a few months.

After the day of celebration, I chose to head north again and work with Search and Rescue as in my heart I still wanted to make it as a winchman.

Before I knew it, I was back down in the South continuing my aircrew training. I had met someone and when I left her behind I really missed her. She didn't know what made me tick, she had no clue of my past and but most of all for the first time we had lots of fun together. Despite the distance I found myself driving to Aberdeen from Lincoln on weekends, not getting there until the early hours of Saturday morning and having to leave mid-afternoon on Sunday. It felt nice to have someone. I felt almost normal, the darkness was a distant memory in my past.

Air Load Master training was intense at an academic level and I found it hard. I have never learned well from books. I need to be shown how to do things then I can get on with them. Despite this I managed to get my wish granted. I was to be streamed onto helicopter aircraft, this was one step closer to becoming a winchman. More training was to follow but this time it was thankfully more practically based.

In the end, I just had a survival course to pass and then I would be off. This proved to be a hurdle as I had a problem in my head. I felt I was out of shape, so I took a lot of supplements, protein shakes and creatine.

When a few extra pounds developed, I would take diet supplements or just wouldn't hold my food down after I ate. I am not sure where this weight fixation came from. Was it from bodybuilding?

I felt good about myself physically. I looked in the mirror and liked the person I saw. I felt strong in the knowledge I could push so hard and that when others looked at me they thought I was strong.

For the training itself, we were in the field with no food, unless we caught it, and with mundane tasks to do, like building shelters and making survival fires.

What is the point in it? If we were shot down behind enemy lines I wasn't going to need to be Robinson Crusoe and be able to build a nice camp, not with modern technology and locating satellites that would spot you from one of your emergency beacons. If I was at war, I wanted to be able to get the fuck out quick, the fitter I was the better.

I lasted two days without my usual volley of supplements and food; I ended up collapsing and having to spend a day in hospital. I was humiliated and sent back to my unit, I had finally failed at something and I hated myself for it.

How did I fail? Was I weak?

All these years I had been strong and a few days of no food and now I was in hospital. I felt pathetic, I was ashamed of myself, I would not fail again.

The day after been released from hospital, I had to visit the military doctor. He wanted a blow by blow account of how I led my life. I told him about all the supplements and training, but I never told him why. Besides he never asked and wasn't interested. All he was interested in was me making it as aircrew. His advice was I had to start drinking more booze and eating a normal unhealthy diet. Guinness and chips then?

At this point, he highlighted to me I had an addiction. The problem with all this sport and exercise had made me an endorphin junky. This guy was choice, he didn't care about the cause, just the symptom. I was waiting for his next advice, but it never came.

I left the doc's in a daze. I was addicted, what was the real addiction though? Was it the need to feel pain, to suppress my past and the darkness?

With my failure of the survival course, the rumour mill at the base exploded. The banter was harsh but I just sucked it up, let them go for it. I knew that eventually they will give up and turn on their next victim. No one here knew how I could snap, they hadn't seen my darkness, they didn't know what I could do.

I had conversations with some about past sports and they knew about my martial arts background, but they didn't know I had the power to switch off. They didn't know about my history, all I had to do was to unlock my past, let in the darkness that would show them.

A few months passed and the doc didn't follow up on

my addiction. I cut out the supplements, but I still trained daily or twice a day. My new relationship was still going strong despite the distance. We seemed to get on as I just didn't have to explore my past with her. Being in the north of Scotland, allowed me to be someone else and it gave me an excuse not to go home.

The weekends I did end up going home were OK as I didn't stay long. A night was all I could really stomach before I felt the need to run and to get away from the place.

Dad moved out of the house which had been my childhood haunt to a council bungalow. Despite his transplant, he was better but never right. He knew how to play on it though, especially if the subject of work appeared. I appreciated he couldn't work, but claiming he needed his wife as a carer was a bit much. She could have gone out got a job and eased his financial burden. Dad started to acknowledge the friction between me and his wife, so if I ever told him I was going back he would arrange time just for us two. We would do lunch or have a pint.

I would always try to get him away from the house as being there all the time couldn't help but affect his mood. If I had a few spare quid, I would send it his way, just to try to ease things a little for him.

The second survival course arrived, this time there was to be no failure, I wouldn't allow it. I ended up passing with no problems. The weather was harsh compared to the last time, piles of ice and snow, this drove me on even though people were dropping out right, left and centre.

I was soon away, posted to further training at RAF Shawbury to the helicopter school. Finally some flying and time to learn how to do the job. Another 12 months loomed, but I would not fail, not again.

Learning to be a crewman is intense. It is not just a case of opening and closing doors. There's meteorology, navigation, learning how to carry different equipment both inside and underneath the aircraft and voice marshalling all key basic skills to learn.

It was a literally a buzz flying around, but the most important thing you had to teach yourself when flying, is to leave your baggage behind. When I put on my helicopter helmet and walked for an aircraft that was it. It didn't matter what had gone on in the past, at home or on the phone to the girlfriend.

All that mattered was the aircraft and that training sortie. Everything else had to wait for my return. It was another way of escaping from it, but this time self punishment wasn't involved.

When you complete the course you are posted to one of the RAF helicopter fleet. It isn't really your choice, the instructors take your personality into account but mainly the RAF decide where they need people. The fleet is small. It is either, Chinook, Puma, Wessex's or Sea King on the Search and Rescue.

I still had a strong desire for Search and Rescue but something else came up. There was a new side of me to explore.

I had a chance of doing some operational tours away from the UK putting my skills to the test in an unfriendly environment. I would do a couple of tours, gain experience, get the need for war out of my system before applying for my dream of Search and Rescue.

I had met a few good guys from the Chinook and the job sounded like I would fit in. The pure size and nature of the Chinook role meant the job was a little more physical, I wanted to be a part of it.

This was a decision which was to shape the rest of my life.

# CHAPTER FOURTEEN

# OOPS INDEED

I arrived at RAF Odiham in December 2000; we had the usual briefings from the Chief Instructor, the do's and don'ts. Like we were young aircrew sergeants and the Sergeants' Mess was to be respected. Tell me something I didn't know!

He then went into the course detail. We were now to undertake a further training course. We had our basic crewman skills and now we were to be taught about the Chinook. More in depth engineering, more in depth voice marshalling. More loading skills both inside and underneath as the Chinook can carry a massive amount of equipment or people and, most exciting of all, door gunnery.

Everything we had learnt was just the foundations. We were about to build the first floor of our proper aircrew careers with the operational conversion course. It was another six months, the only down side it wasn't to start until March 2001.

He explained when we passed out to our squadrons we wouldn't have the opportunity to take masses of leave. It was best to get rid of any accumulated leave now. As I had come through the ranks and re-signed a contract for 22 years, I had loads of leave to take. So much so, I ended up filing in a leave pass until the start of the course, three months later.

My leave was spent in Aberdeen with my girlfriend living at her rented place, after a month we were still getting on great and I proposed. I don't know why, it was sort of expected, when I look back I am unsure if I loved her but I felt away from it all up there. It was like my safety zone. All my family got on really well with her as I did with hers, so it seemed like a good idea at the time.

Being engaged, we decided to look for a place to buy. We soon found a great flat and decided to go for it. We were to be married so we had to trust each other. It was strange to try to trust someone. I felt vulnerable, unnerved. I was letting someone close to me. I could get hurt.

The pain and darkness of the past was buried away in a corner of my head. I still trained hard, this was my life's constant, my equilibrium, a way to regain my balance, now I was beginning to look to the future, the past only returned if I returned to Yorkshire.

Before I could blink, it was time to head back to the South to prepare myself for the hardest flying course and toughest part of my new career. I was back at Odiham attached to 18 Squadron, Operational Conversation Flight. Now it was the real thing. There was a lot to learn, flying rules and regulations, loading regulations and engineering, before the techniques and checks associated with actually operating in the aircraft. It was a busy time, too busy to really think about things.

The Chinook has two pilots and generally two crewmen. When you go through training, you have instructors with you to teach and asses you on every trip. You change instructors every few weeks so you get a more objective view on how you are progressing.

One of the instructors was notorious for trying to fail at least one student per course as this kept the others on their toes. We had completed the basic phase and were moving to a more advanced stage of training and it was my turn for him.

Trouble came my way on a navigation sortie. We had been out for hours and the pilot instructor like the rest of the crew was drained, we had taxied the aircraft back to the parking spots at the front of the squadron. In the back were just me and the instructor. I had been navigational assisting for the last four hours, while my instructor was monitoring the engineering systems and me.

Before you start closing down Chinook, the front crewman, unties the aircraft chocks, releases his safety harness, jumps out of the front door and chocks the aircraft, ready for stopping the rotors.

The pilot places the parking brake on to lock the aircrafts wheels and starts the procedures ready to close down the engines and rotors. This time things went wrong, the pilot forgot to move from holding the collective lever. This is the lever which puts power to the engines and lifts the aircraft off the ground, this is on the left hand side just like a car handbrake. The Chinook parking brake is forward of this lever

Today the pilot made a mistake, the collective was pulled rapidly, I was bending down getting the chocks. Before we knew it my head hit the roof, the aircraft jumped into the air rapidly. The pilot realised what happened and violently put the aircraft back onto the ground. I went from hitting the roof to hitting a metal strip on the floor in the rear, impacting both knees very hard.

The pain shot through my knees, I knew instantly they were damaged but my training told me to get on with the job. I looked down the aircraft checking to see if the instructor was OK as he had lost his balance.

The pilot crackled over the intercom, giggling, "Oops sorry about that."

Not "Is everyone OK?" I noticed.

I righted myself, I could feel my knees pulsating but the adrenaline was rushing. I got the chocks, jumped down and placed them at the front wheel, trying to get back in to the aircraft. A hot pain went through my knees, they had taken a big impact. I was to learn later, a crewman was walking behind the aircraft and saw it happen; we had got to around seven feet in the aircraft and then rapidly hit the ground, violently shuddering the aircraft. 'Oops' indeed.

We debriefed the sortie; the pilot decided there was no need to report the incident through the flight safety chain as it was just one of those things. The day was done I headed back to the Sergeants' Mess and my room, the pain was sharp. I closed my eyes and put it away, I kept telling myself to use the pain, use it like I know how. My knees were really swollen so I got some ice and elevated them as I didn't want to go to the sick bay.

The next day I had another training sortie. A favourite saying among Chinook crewman was, 'Dry your eyes and get on with it.'

The next morning I was no better but despite the pain and swelling I went on the training sortie, I was still drying my eyes.

I was in the rear of the aircraft; the trainee pilots were practising a manoeuvre to land the aircraft in a short space of ground. That day I was down the rear of the aircraft, kneeling on the seat, so I could keep lookout too the left and behind. We hit the ground hard, all my weight jerked forward onto my knees, crashing into the metal bar under the seat. I screamed with pain, it was over, I had to put my hands up. I could hardly straighten them, the aircraft captain cancelled the sortie and we returned to base. I made an appointment with sick bay.

I reported to the medical officer and it was an instant

two weeks of non-flying. I was going to be behind and faced the threat of being put onto the course starting in six months time. It would have been a real failure if this was to happen and I couldn't let it.

I received a big dressing down from the instructor, who was flying with me when the pilot made a mistake. He went on about how I should be able to take the hits and I break too easy. If he only knew.

I stared blindly back at him, but that fuelled him more, I was doing it for his sake though because his words were hitting me inside and I had to keep control. If I caved in I knew the darkness would leak back into my head again. This guy was gunning for me. Was I going to be the one he re-coursed to send his message to the Chinook world?

Two weeks later after a course of physio and Ibuprofen. I was scheduled to fly again on the day my sick note ran out, I had already informed the staff I had a doctor's appointment that morning to check the state of my fitness for my knees, but that didn't matter to the instructor. He planned to fly me before my appointment.

I refused to fly and that gave him the fuel he needed. I went to the doctor. I knew the outcome before it was said; my knees were still swollen to allow me in the air, so another fortnight off. I knew this was going to mean failure and I would be pushed back to the next course. I began to hate myself, I had promised never to fail again and here it was it was happening again.

I went back to the squadron dejected, waiting for the inevitable to happen. Before I could even find the crewman boss to discuss it, he was my chain of command, I was tannoyed to report to the Instructors' Office and my favourite notorious instructor.

He was smiling. I could sense it coming. He took me to a private briefing room and then he presented to me, with the biggest grin, an official ground report for refusing to fly. I was gobsmacked, it was like being sucker punched and knocked onto the canvas, that feeling off disbelief.

I only refused because according to regulations you need to get the all clear from the doctor to fly again. He sat there and kept smiling. I could feel the emotions well up inside.

I was made to sign the ground report and it would be on my record. In that very moment, he had turned the key to the box in my head, the box which held my darkness at bay, it was open again and seeping out.

Sod them, I knew what I had to do. I got my training kit, the weights bay, I pushed my upper body, harder stronger, the feelings of hate of myself for failing were driving me to the edge. I felt it go, my nose burst, my blood pressure was through the roof and with it the pressure had to release. It felt good, I looked in the mirror, I smiled at what I saw, the blood running down my face. Only one thing for it, I thought, an extra set or two. I could still go to the edge and beyond.

# CHAPTER FIFTEEN

# THE KEY TO A BOX

When I returned to the squadron it felt different. I was still hobbling around the place. My colleagues appeared to look through me and when I went into rooms, conversations stopped. Were they talking about me? There was no room for sick weak aircrew.

I headed for the Chief crewman's office, looking for a job, I wanted some way of still been involved within the squadron, I still wanted to be a part of the team.

His door was closed. I stood at ease to the side of the door, there were voices inside. It sounded like an instructor meeting. Usually I would have come back later, but then I heard it, my instructors voice and my name, I stood now intent on listening what was been said.

I was being called a malingerer and there was nothing wrong with me. I thought, so this guy is a fucking doctor now. He sat there and bitched about me and it hurt. I wanted to burst in and just beat the crap out of him, but I listened on, the Chief instructor took over, saying I would be re-coursed and official action with a ground warning had already been issued.

I'd forgotten about the ground warning and the piece of

paper I was made sign. If you get three, that's it, goodbye to your aircrew career and probably my military career too.

With this further failure, my head was running a million miles an hour, how do I to stop that? I went to the health and safety officer. If things were to be covered up about the accident, I was going to uncover them and cover my arse.

My sick note ran out and I was made temporally unfit for duty for six months. I was to be re-coursed, I had failed, so my instructor had the last laugh, but that wasn't enough for him he had to twist the knife. He had arranged that I would be sent away from the squadron to an IT support job elsewhere on the base. This is unheard of. If you are sick aircrew you do a desk job, tasking, planning or operations. You are kept within your squadron, you are never sent away.

With a smile he told me. I wanted to pick up the chair and batter him with it. I just stood and listened. I began to drift, his lips were moving but I couldn't hear him, blank him, don't snap, look through, look beyond. If I had taken his stare, I would have turned the key and let the dark out of its box.

I was cast out to the wilderness of an IT support job for eight months but I knew I'd be back to prove my worth.

The frustration of my knees and the pressure I put on myself not to fail began to leak into my relationship. I cared but I wasn't showing it particularly well. My fiancée was starting to distance herself from me too.

I decided the phone wouldn't do, I had to see her face to face, so unannounced I went home.

I cannot remember why the argument started, but it did and she had a fiery temper, especially if she had a drink, tonight was to be one of those days. I just took whatever she could throw at me verbally, nothing mattered, I was strong. The next day, I invaded her privacy and checked her phone, text message inbox and sent messages. There was a lot to one particular guy and the texts were far from innocent? Two and two made four, I got my coat and went for a walk.

I had to get out I could feel it inside starting to churn up again, was she cheating on me? It certainly seemed that way, I needed to confront her with it, so I did. It was red rag to a bull though and she focused on the fact I had invaded her private life.

I was marrying this girl and it was obvious what she was doing, it was a test to control my feelings. I could feel it all going off inside my heart and my head, but I remained calm, just take it, she couldn't hurt me.

If she was seeing someone else, I had warned them, they either took it underground or stopped either way I didn't care too much. It really didn't matter, what she did, I had bigger things happening in my life. What troubled me more was the fact I was failing at another relationship. What was wrong with me?

I tried to give them all what they wanted; I tried to be the knight in shining armour. Was it that I was trying too hard or was it me? Why should I let them in my head, any of them? My head is my private space, I had to save them all from it. My darkness wasn't to be shared. I didn't want to fail again. I couldn't do it too myself, so I pretended it didn't happen.

I accepted her explanation and put it out of my head, but I didn't trust her. She would have to earn that again, if she could. So I went off the rails; they were all objects again, women, I started to slip back to my past; two wrongs never made a right; I justified it by reverting to my old self. Out with the guys, seeing what conquests you could get. Inside I hated it, it was all meaningless. When I looked in the mirror, I loathed the person staring back. What was I becoming?

Our wedding was looming and I wanted to go through

with it, I wanted to conform to the normal; wife, job, home and 2.4 children. That's what people expected, that's what I was hoping would help me bury my past and finally throw away the key to the box where my darkness lived.

The wedding was booked but now clashed with the start of my new flying course. In the end it didn't matter as during a night of madness on my stag night, I ended in hospital having two wrist operations. This stopped me from starting the course for a further six months.

Another failure. They were starting to add up, what was I doing? The wedding passed without incident. My Dad even surprised me by taking me to one side and thanking me for all the help I had given him through the years. But now I had my own wife to look after and I needed to focus on her, not him.

I didn't know how to feel, it wasn't a fresh start, but it was the start of a new future with my wife. I had seen enough divorces and arguments. This wouldn't happen to us, we wouldn't fail at our marriage. I wanted this to work, but inside I knew it wasn't quite right; both of us had been playing around. We should have called it a day back then, but I ended up saying, "I do."

I was going to give it my all, no matter what came my way. The key had been turned and my darkness was locked in its box. For now at least.

# Chapter Sixteen

# HOOK, LINE AND STARES

So six months of relative married bliss elapsed and I was to join the operation conversion course, for my second attempt. The marriage was going OK, mainly as we were still living apart. I tried to get back on weekends to Aberdeen but some weeks I was just too busy or it was too expensive. In retrospect, it was probably the wrong way to start married life.

I was one of the few guys to have a private phone line installed in my room in the Sergeants' Mess. Ironically I had it so I could keep in better contact with my wife. We had discussed moving south but I thought it was best if I got the course out of the way. Along with the phone came an Internet connection. I let people use it when I wasn't there as, every night between 7pm and 9pm I was in the gym religiously. I left my door open and people could use my stuff. We were all Sergeants, all a part of the same team. My emotions were pretty much in check, the darkness was locked away, things were going well; the flying course, my marriage, Dad was in a better place. I was being careful of my knees.

Three months into the course, I was progressing well, some of the staff had changed and we had a new instructor who was just finding his feet. We were about to get checked by our external examiners. With aircrew, the checks come on a very regular basis to keep you on top of your game. This is one reason why we have the best air force in the world. We had just completed an underslung load sortie and the centre hook of the aircraft needed to be reset. It could only be done by a qualified crewman, we were tight on time and the instructor was rushing, telling me I should be quicker. I pointed out that the hook needed to be reset. If I had done like he wanted, we would have damaged the aircraft. To me it was about team work, we all looked out for each other.

The next day the training was search and rescue. Being winched from the side of the Chinook, with it's massive downwash, is a completely different experience to the other helicopters I had been winched from. The new instructor was being checked at the same time. The procedures for putting a live body on the winch wire are stringent. The first time you use it, you always check the winch's integrity before putting a person on it. If is going to fail chances are it would fail on the first winch. For this reason, you attached yourself by a safety harness to the aircraft and clip onto the winch to prove the winch works before releasing your safety harness.

The instructor told me to go to the door without my safety harness, this was the first time it had been used and it was yet to be checked. I refused as it was dangerous. This led to a 'discussion' and I refused to give in, I knew I was right. The discussion morphed into a full blown argument. This is a big no no, in a live aircraft as communication can't break down. I constantly refused and, in the end, the sortie got cancelled and we returned to the squadron. We were both fuming with each other. What sort of instructor was he? He was fuming with me because his full instructor ticket was likely to be delayed. We always debriefed every sortie, this one was short and sharp, my procedures were correct.

My rule was what happens at work stays at work. When you leave, never take it back home with you. This was my safety strategy. If I could do this it would keep my balance, my box locked, I had to keep my already cluttered brain from any extra bad thoughts. So I headed for my daily gym routine so I could disconnect from the day. On the way there I bumped into the instructor, we had a chat. I felt there was no problems between us, he seemed chirpy and straight about things. He knew I was heading to the gym and asked if he could use my Internet connection. I said of course he could; what harm could it do?

The next day, another training sortie was planned and we were just walking to the aircraft when one of the guys from the course came running out with his helmet.

He called me over, "Get to the Crewman Leader's office, its important."

I looked confused, "Can it wait? I'm off flying."

"Not this time mate, I'm taking your place. You have to get there now."

My brain went into overdrive there was only one reason you got taken off flying, something serious had happened to one of my close family. Was it my wife, Dad, Mum, Grandma? What could be wrong?

I sprinted in with the aircraft starting up behind me. I dropped my flying kit in and headed up the three floors to the Crewman Leader's office. His door was open. He shared the office with the squadron leader in charge of the operational conversion flight.

"Sergeant, come in!" I could tell this was serious as usually it was first name terms.

I walked into the office, my head was racing but now confused, why had he used rank? As I entered, the door was closed behind me, I was startled and looked around. A guy in a suit had closed it - average height, cheap suit. Next to the squadron leader was another one. I started to feel threatened, why was this prick blocking my exit? Why had he closed the door?

The one by the officer started to speak "Sergeant we are arresting you for having paedo images of children on your PC."

"What?"

The guy in the suit repeated himself; I answered this time. "What is that? I don't understand?"

He changed his statement. "You are being arrested for having indecent pictures of children on your PC."

It registered this time and my head started to spin. I was falling into a black hole. I had done what? No way, not me. What the hell? What was happening?

The chief crewman asked if I wanted a seat. Maybe the colour had drained from my face. I did feel sick, a sickness so deep, you will know if you have ever felt it.   I had to take control and get a grip.

I looked the guy straight in the eye, "You must be fucking joking!"

My language was all over the place. I felt it was pointless being nice with. I was hurt, my emotions were everywhere. He spoke again introducing himself and his colleagues, two corporals from PNSS - the military's Special Branch!

This was real, this was happening. My head was awash with different emotions, the sickness grew deeper as I thought about what I was accused of.

In a moment of straight thinking, I turned to the squadron leader, "Sir, I formally request you are my airman's friend."

He looked shocked I had just dragged him into it. I remembered from being arrested in training you could have anyone as an airman's friend and I chose him.  He was now responsible in making sure all procedures were followed. My head went somewhere else again, it was hard to stay focused. I had to get control of it.

The Suit started moving towards me. I jumped up, everyone stood off.

My head was clear. "I cannot have you hand cuffing me. Shit sticks. If this leaves this office, I will be accused of being a kiddy fiddler for ever. I haven't done anything, I promise you. You have my full cooperation, but please be sensitive to this allegation. Who else knows?"

The Suit said, "The Station Commander, the officer in charge of the police, my Wing Commander and the two in the office. They all promise to be discrete."

I started to spin again; we agreed I would go with in their car. We left the office and the corridor had the usual buzz of people. Every stare burned even though no one was really looking at me. We had suits around the place all the time but I was already thinking everyone had found me guilty, despite knowing I had done nothing wrong.

The police flight was at the other side of the airfield, I was in their car. I had options to run, but that meant I was guilty. I could fight my way out, they were both up front. I had child locks, but I could punch one out and then take the other, they were not armed.

Fortunately, my sensible head took over. We went through the back door at the police flight, straight to the interview room where I was cautioned properly. Every time they gave me something to read, I couldn't, the letters spun on the page. I gave it to the squadron leader, my airman's friend. Boy I needed him here, I could have signed anything. After the formal caution they explained it was time to search my room in the Sergeants' Mess.

When we got there, they went straight to my PC and monitor. As it would look bad if they walked out with loads of evidence bags, I gave them a military holdall. My brain drifted in and out, throughout the search, I was constantly asking them how this had happened. They didn't answer at first.

Eventually they started to chat when they saw I was cooperating. I was trying to make it as painless for everyone as I could; it was to be a full search. I emptied a cupboard with a few porno mags and videos. After all I was away from my Mrs; it wasn't uncommon in the forces. They were bagged.

I had a stack of music CD's. I loved music, they looked at the shelf with them all on, "Have you got anything hidden in there?"

"No," I answered; so they moved on.

I logged flying duties in diaries and notebooks; in the back I had passwords for banks and websites like BT, these were to be confiscated too. When they asked to see something, I just got it, I had nothing to hide. I was back in control, the search started to become comical, one copper sat on my chair thumbing magazines, one pointing to cupboards. They asked what was in them. I was organised I hated not been able to find things, I'd list what was in the cupboards, they opened them; they didn't move anything. Everything was how I described it, if I remembered I had a diary or anything, I instantly got it for them. I wanted this over quickly.

When it was eventually over, they agreed to leave in front of me and I could carry the holdall with all the evidence to the car. It looked like I was packing for weekend leave. We got back to the interview room, everything was logged and I was released pending further investigation.

Lunch time came and went, no way could I eat my appetite was lost. I had an hour, only one thing for it, I got my runners. I knew my knee would play up and it would give me pain and at that moment I needed pain. It would keep the darkness sealed in my head even though it was already seeping out. I needed to run away from it. I knew a secluded route, I got into the fields, good no one around, I fell to my knees, I no longer had control of my emotions, no one was around. I could afford to be weak, tears started to stream, I couldn't believe what had happened.

It then happened, as clear as a cloudless sky, the inner voice in my head, "Get up, run!" So I did, the combination of the pain in my knee and running again, the stress finally hit home. I felt it welling up inside, I was sick; "Keep running" the voice within urged me, I was sick again.

When there was nothing left my head turned to a new thought, what will my wife think? Would I lose her? What about my best mate? What would my parents think? Why should I care what my parents thought? Things were as normal as could be between us, I had moved on so had they. I owed them a little respect to tell them.

I got back to the mess, trying to avoid everyone. Every time I saw someone, I thought they knew. Their eyes burnt deep inside me. I cleaned myself up, put my game face back on and headed back to work. I went straight to the Crewman Leaders office, we closed the door and I just let it all out.

I explained I was confused, I hadn't done anything, he tried to reassure me. He said when they explained why I was arrested, he saw it in my face, he knew I wasn't guilty. He offered to suspend me until this was all cleared up. I said no way; I needed something normal, if I stopped flying, I would go crazy. In the end, he agreed and told me to take the day off.

I got back to my room it was time to call people. I checked my watch, my wife wouldn't be home. She had to hear it first, I owed her that. I needed her input as this could affect her too. My stomach was telling me it was empty and my nausea had subsided. The thought of dining with my colleagues churned me up again. What if someone had seen? What if someone had let it slip?

I couldn't face them, not yet; so I went to Tesco. As I walked through the car park, I was hyper-alert. I walked down one of the food aisles, then it happened, a young girl ran in front of me, I froze. She looked at me, I couldn't move, a tear rolled down my cheek, then another, then the basket fell from my hand. She turned and went back to her mum.

I ran out of the store, tears streaming down my face, I couldn't face looking at a child, any child. I felt I was dirty, everyone around me must know. I must look like someone who gets off by hurting children. I hated myself, the box in my head exploded, the darkness no longer seeped out, it was now free.

I got back to my room, the hunger had left, water from my tap would suffice; it was time to make that call. I shook as I dialled the numbers, when my wife answered and she had given me the low down on her day, it was just easier to listen than to speak. I started to tell her, trying to explain what had happened. She was speechless but who wouldn't be? Your husband arrested, accused of having indecent pictures of children. I could tell she wanted off the phone, I think it needed to sink in.

I had started now, I may as well get it over with. I dialled all the other people. They all held the same disbelief and I was relieved they all believed in me. They knew I hadn't done it. Not long after my wife called back to chat some more. This time she was comforting and reassuring. I needed her to be.

I said I was coming home that weekend despite the cost, I needed away from here. I was heading for a sleepless night, my brain constantly churning asking the questions.

Why and how? Not just for this but everything before this. My brain was awash with it all, there was only one thing I could do, I put on my sports kit on, it was the early hours. I grabbed my gym card and headed for the weights room. There I maybe able to make sense of it.

The next day I had to face my course colleagues. I didn't have to explain anything, no one questioned it. They had been told I had had a personal drama that I had to sort out. I put my game face, on the outside I looked normal, inside I was in bits. Then the tannoy went. I was to report to the Crewman Leader's office, my heart sank, what now?

When I got there it was a pep talk, if I wanted to continue with the course I had to forget about what had happened there was no room for it in the air. If he only knew my history, as soon as that helmet went on, my history stayed firmly on the ground.

The days dragged, the nights were full of turmoil and images of the past. My only escape was the gym or when I was in the air. Every other time I was consumed with my darkness. When I was at the base, I no longer went out. I started to avoid friends and family who had children. When I saw a child I felt dirty, I felt everyone knew and judged me. I would look into people's eyes and I would see it there.

# CHAPTER SEVENTEEN

# STITCHED UP

It was December, months had already passed since I was arrested and there was a talk of war. Iraq was on the horizon and planning and training the crews was priority. Things were beginning to get the better of me, concentration was poor. I was scraping by; my evenings plagued with bad thoughts. Every time it ended the same way with me pushing my boundaries in the gym.

My relationship with my wife was being affected. I was stressed out, little things were upsetting me and my sex drive was non-existent. I was talking of never wanting a family. I was beginning to keep her away, in my head I was doing her a favour. If I disconnected I could protect her from darkness.

Obviously there was something wrong and they were preparing a case against me. I was expecting the worst, even though I had done nothing wrong. Newspapers are full of wrongly accused people especially those who have been accused of this. I made a decision on Monday I would see the chief crewman and remove myself from training; it was the safest thing to do for the crews and the aircraft.

When I walked into the office he knew what was coming, it was in my face. I couldn't cope anymore, he told me to keep going and he would start making phone calls to see what the delay was. The next day I was called back to his office, he told me to sit down. My stomach was churning, my arms were shaking, I put my head in my hands, I was a broken man.

"I have spoken with PNSS, they say there was something in your 'Favourites', but it wasn't linked to anything. There are no charges to answer. You will be released and everything returned to you."

My eyes started to fill, the odd tear trickled down my cheek, I couldn't control it. He stood, handed me a tissue and said, "There is the phone, now phone your family and tell them the nightmare is over."

Despite being released my dreams were still plagued with past events, not just recent ones, but ones I thought I had buried deep inside. During the days, burning questions I needed answers to flooded my head. How had it happened? Why had it happened to me?

I still felt unclean, no shower could wash this away, it was engrained. I still couldn't face children, it just didn't feel right and the thought of starting a family of my own was now a distant dream.

February arrived and I was summoned to the police flight for the official release and my belongings were returned. I knew the releasing officer, the questions were still burning inside me, the how's and why's? I tried to bring them up in the official taped release, but I was cut short.

I was given some advice, check my favourites and always lock my door and password everything. I rushed back to the mess and set up my system. I needed to know. I had IT skills and knew my way around systems. I could tell what the police had done, where they had searched, restoring the drive to an earlier version to see if I had deleted anything and then restored it to how it was when I handed it over.

In front of me was my Internet Explorer Favourites list

and in it, there was the title Child Porn. I looked at the link, there were no web addresses; just www. I set about searching for a date and time in the History, I found one. The night before my arrest, the time I was in the gym. I always trained at that time, who had done this?

The flying course finished mid-March, most of the squadron had deployed in readiness for the Iraq war; it was a quite place to be. We had a celebration lunch in the Officers' Mess, we were now limited-combat ready crewmen. This meant we were trusted alone in certain missions but needed further on the job training in advanced tactics and flying techniques to achieve a combat ready state. The life of aircrew was constant checks and more checks.

The lunch was a social affair and then the speeches started and I was awarded the prize of best crewman on the course. For one second, everything fell away, the darkness subdued, it felt good. When we broke for the bar, people we congratulating me, then it happened, the burning question was about to be answered.

An instructor shook my hand and said praisingly, "You have done brilliantly, considering what you have been through."

It was like hitting a brick wall, for a second I was being normal, then I was back to the troubled dark times. I looked at him, I was confused how could he know, "How do you know about it, there is only a handful of people who should know about that, best you start talking."

He knew he had dropped a clanger, he started to speak he didn't have a choice, if he didn't talk I would take it further, I needed answers. He explained how he came into work on the day I was arrested, to find the instructor I had 'discussions' with when we were in the air looking troubled. They were friends and he said he had found something on my PC and needed to know what to do; they decided they had to call in the police.

I had stopped listening, I now knew who it was, it all made sense, I had seen him on my way out to the gym, outside the mess, he asked me if he could use my PC. With the new information I checked the bar, he wasn't here, he was on the deployment ready for the Iraqi war. I wanted revenge, he had cost me a lot, I wanted him to hurt like I was. My past flooded in he had to be punished, not today but some time in the future. I had time to think it over find the best time to inflict maximum damage, how could I hurt him?

Would I find peace in doing it or would I just hate myself even more?

# CHAPTER EIGHTEEN

# THE CALL

It was time to try to make a proper go at our marriage, we agreed to get a military married quarter and live together in the South. This was something we hadn't ever done. It was a daunting prospect but I wanted to feel normal after the turbulent past few months.

These last few months had changed me, the scars were beginning to show. I was becoming less understanding. When things needed discussing I would avoid conflict at all costs. I either headed to the gym or buried myself with work. It was my way to keep the peace. I wanted the darkness to leave for a while, but it wouldn't. That little voice inside started to question things, my reflection in a mirror looked angry or sad. The nights were full of long constant dreams of my past again haunting me.

The war in Iraq had begun and was in full swing. Friends and colleagues from 18 Squadron were at the forefront of it. Despite being a part of the squadron, we had just qualified so we were left behind this time. My thoughts of revenge had subsided, I didn't have concrete evidence. I had only one guy's word about how it had happened and this wasn't enough to justify hurting someone, so I hurt myself. I used the pain from the incident to fuel my darkness and push my body to new limits. My head was starting to feel full, little things seemed to bother me. I couldn't let go and the more I tried, the more I held on.

The guys returned from the front line, everyone was back safe. Another squadron had gone out to take over, we were going to continue this rolling change like that for the next few years, every 10-12 weeks. I was excited about the fact I was going to get my chance to go to a war zone. First though, I was to take a trip to the Falklands which was a great place to train new crews.

After I returned I found myself volunteering for short notice detachments around the world. Anything to keep me busy. If I was busy I could stop it.

It was nearly my turn to ship out for a tour of Iraq. Dad and his wife came to see us. Now I could tolerate her in small doses. Something had changed inside me maybe I was growing up or maybe the new stuff in my head now outweighed what had happened in my childhood. It no longer mattered as it made my Dad's life easier and with it my life easier.

My wife got what she wanted, cars, holidays, jewellery, it didn't matter. I wanted her happy and I thought if I couldn't give her me, material things would be a good replacement. We had a barbecue and had too many beers, Dad's emotions were running high as I was off to a war zone but it didn't bother me.

It wasn't that volatile out there yet, but to him it was a big deal. We were chatting late into the night and then he stunned me. He asked me outright that if anything happened to him would I look out for his wife?

I don't know why, maybe the booze, maybe it was I was about to deploy to Iraq. I was shocked as I heard my words leave my lips, I promised him I would. Anything just to give him the inner peace he was looking for.

The next morning goodbyes were said, they went home

to leave us for our last night together before my deployment. I was wired, it wasn't the romantic evening my wife wanted or deserved. I checked my kit, packed, unpacked, re-checked, I wanted to make sure my first operational detachment went without a hitch. The next day, I was picked up by the bus at the married quarters, inside I was excited, I wanted to use all the training I had been given.

The deployment to Iraq went without hitch. It was quite an experience. We were rocketed and mortared at the bases. You felt the shudders. Our job was to transport casualties to field hospitals. Shots were fired at us but this was nothing unusual. The majority of the Iraqi population were glad to see us, especially in the South. Most came and waved and there were only the odd few insurgents who wanted to stir things up.

We had a variety of missions. One night we found ourselves taking people into Baghdad, we usually didn't visit the red zone but tonight we had to. It mostly went without incident but we had a scare when an American Blackhawk got his airfield procedures wrong and came at us head to head. There was nothing we could do, thankfully he saw us in time.

It was a big learning curve, I had to make choices, split second decisions for real and there could be consequences if I got it wrong. A part of a crewman's war role is to man the M60 weapon. We were flying down a canal when we spotted two Iraqi teens, not more than 15 years, one had an AK-47. He levelled it at the aircraft. Do I shoot or don't I? As I readied the weapon, I began to squeeze the trigger, the decision buzzing, his friend luckily jumped in front of him. I released the pressure on the trigger, no shots were fired.

We landed not far down the banking, deployed our onboard troops and they disarmed him. He was lucky. I should have shot but I called to the pilot to turn away from the threat and his friend had the sense to jump in front. My inner sense also told me not to shoot.

All in all, I enjoyed being there. For once I felt I was achieving something useful and that I was a part of something meaningful. In a war zone, I had found an inner peace, the darkness was contained in a box and that box didn't travel with me to this place. It couldn't, I wouldn't allow it. All I was concerned about was getting the job done and everybody coming home safe. I just had the strange feeling that I didn't care if it was me who didn't ever return home.

When we did arrive home safe, it was not long before Christmas. I was still on a high from the tour and nothing seemed to trouble me to the same degree as it had before. On my wife's day off, we went to Yorkshire to do the dutiful thing and see everyone, tell the stories and hand out Christmas presents. We only could stay a day and that was more than enough.

Christmas itself was all planned out, the in-laws were coming down and my Mum and her husband were joining us for Boxing Day. A couple of days before, Dad phoned me as he had a PC problem. When I had been back for the day I found it full of viruses, so I cleaned it up and gave him a lecture on how to stay protected online. Probably a bit ironic coming from me.

Christmas Day arrived and I phoned Dad to wish him all the best, his wife answered. We chattered and she told me dad hadn't got out of bed yet he was complaining of indigestion. This wasn't uncommon so I told her to get him to give me a call if he got up and I heard nothing for the rest of the day.

On Boxing Day, Mum and her husband arrived for yet another day of food and booze. I wasn't feeling great and I hadn't had a lot to drink the day before. I had a knot in my stomach and I felt nauseous. I phoned Dad, again the answer was the same, no change from yesterday. I suggested the doctor but Dad didn't want to bother him.

I nursed one can of Guinness all day, my stomach was all over the place; despite having guests I made my excuses and went to bed early. The phone woke me up at 11.45pm. Everyone had called it a night and were in bed. I checked caller display 'Dad Home', and answered. I knew straight away it wasn't good news, it was my uncle.

"There is no easy way of telling you this, but your Dad is really ill."

My heart sank, "How ill?"

"Well, the paramedics are with him."

"What's the problem?"

It was surreal my training took over; I needed facts, I was medically trained and I needed to know.

"He has had a heart attack."

"How bad, what are the paramedics doing, are they using the defibrillator, have they injected any drugs into him yet? Is the doctor there?"

He stumbled for an answer.

"What are they doing?" I shouted to no avail. I was 200 miles away and useless, the tone of my voice alarmed my wife.

"Have you phoned my sister?"

"Err no, shall I?"

"Don't worry; I'll sort it, I'll phone you back, keep the line clear." I rang off.

I looked at my wife, "Its my Dad, he's having a massive heart attack the paramedics are with him, get your stuff together we are going."

I then turned my attention to the phone, my wife went off to wake everyone. I needed peace, I closed the bedroom door, now was the time for a straight head.

I dialled my sister she lived three miles away from Dad's house, I needed her arse there quick as I needed an honest account. Fortunately she picked up and I gave it to her straight and told her to get there quick.

My hands were beginning to shake, I hit redial, it only rang once before my uncle answered. At least he had kept the line clear.

"What are they doing to him? Is the doctor there?"

"Yes, the doctor is here with him."

For some reason, I already had the answer to my next statement, it was a feeling deep inside, I knew he was gone.

"He's dead isn't he?"

At that very moment, the doctor had pronounced him dead at 0.10am.

"Sorry, yes he is, I'm so sorry."

For years he'd wished for death and for years I had wished it for him, but now we had become friends. I had to be practical, it was pointless being anything else. He was dead, time to sort this shit out, so I told them my sister was on her way and I was about to set off too. As I was chatting with my uncle, I overheard voices in the background, people talking about me, I shouldn't drive up, I wasn't safe. How dare they say that, who the hell did they think they were?

Our conversation soon ended, I was getting angry, everyone's emotions were high, just stay here and leave early, keep the peace. They needed to sort things their end, at my end I had guests to tell, I wanted to chat with my best friend, not my wife, for some reason it had to be him. Despite this feeling I didn't call yet. I went downstairs everyone was up, I stood at the kitchen door, the kettle was on, something like that it's easier just to say it, "He's dead."

A brew came my way and the offer of a whiskey. I didn't want an alcoholic drink, I wanted to get in the car, it felt wrong to be sat here with a brew. What about my Grandma and sister?

Everyone fussed, I was somewhere else, just thinking, my head was spinning out of control. I went into the garage, I dialled my friend's number, he knew something was up as he was more than my friend he was my family. My wife came and hugged me, I was empty, I cannot explain it; numbness had taken my body.

I told everyone that I would be leaving at 6am and my wife was coming with me, there was some resistance, but not much. I handed Mum the keys and apologised, I had to go as I was needed elsewhere.

When everyone was back in bed I just lay awake. People were snoring and my wife was asleep. I started to feel angry, how dare they sleep? The anger grew. It was inside me where that deep nausea hides, I had only experienced this once before, I couldn't hold it down. I ran to the bathroom and puked, I felt ashamed it was probably nothing more than shock, was I weak?

I had to get my strength back, I couldn't be sick, I got my cycling kit and headed for the garage, there in front of me was my bike attached to my indoor turbo trainer. I clipped into the pedals, it was time to ride. I had to be strong, I refuse to be weak, with weakness comes pain. I was pushing hard, my head spinning, I then remembered my last conversation with Dad had been an angry one, over PCs and football. I pushed harder, a text came in, my best friend, did I want him to come down? I didn't need to reply, he was already planning his journey.

The next text was from my sister, was I up? I phoned her while I rode, she had been at Dad's house for hours. Everyone had left, she was upset but had been practical. A dead body expels fluids from various places, she said she couldn't get them out of the bathroom carpet. I told her not to worry, she shouldn't have tried, but it was her way of keeping busy. I asked if anyone had told my Grandma, no one had. I was angry she deserved to be told it was her son, we chatted for ages and when I hung up it was around 5am and I had cycled all night. I went back upstairs and woke my wife, we were soon on the road.

I hit the M1 at speed. I had to get there and tell my Grandma, I owed her that. I got to my Grandma's at the same time as my auntie, uncle and Dad's wife. We all hugged in the street. I knew his wife loved my Dad and I remembered my promise to him months earlier, "If anything ever happens, look after her."

A promise, was a promise. We went into the house as my Grandma was coming downstairs having been woken up with all the commotion. When she saw my face, she knew instantly. Uncle sat her down and between us we told her. Her son had died, she was devastated.

I handed her a brew and got the whiskey out and topped it up. She asked questions like when and how? The answers hurt her as much as the news, nobody had woken her. I was angry with them for that as I knew she was strong and she should have been told immediately. She was devastated, what mother wouldn't be?

She soon wanted left alone to her own thoughts; I respected that and would return later. The day was spent running around various places, telling people the news and being practical. When my Dad's wife was with her family, I returned to Dad's and saw the bathroom carpet was a mess with body fluids. I ripped it out and put it by the bin. I would dispose of it later.

I was tired and didn't want to stay so I went to the pub as I knew my best friend's parents would be there. They were like my parents, they had looked after me as much as anyone else when I was growing up. The serious drinking started as soon my best pal walked in, having just driven nearly 500 miles. It was great he was there, we had beers late into the night. I needed to drink.

The next day I was back to being practical. I had contained my darkness as arrangements had to be made. There never is a good time to die, but during the Christmas period really isn't one of them as so many places were closed. Dad usually did these tasks when other family members died, now it was up to me.

I started to sort through his paperwork and found his wallet. Inside were credit cards, loads of them. I asked his wife if she knew about them, she only knew about one. By the time I finished counting the cards and adding the statements, any feelings of grief were replaced with anger and disbelief. In total, there was around £47,000 of debt. He had been clever not to let on to anyone. His estate was worthless; the house was council; the car was mobility; the minuscule insurance policies would just about pay for his funeral.

The cremation date was set for January so he was laid in the funeral home until then. I took people to see him and I went in and said my goodbyes away from them all. My sadness was replaced with anger, he hadn't told me about his money worries as I could have helped, then I remembered the promise to look after his wife. The anger increased as everyone puts the dead on a pedestal. If they only knew about the past, the debt he had left. I kept quiet around people as I didn't want to take anything away from their grieving process. When they offered support to me, I smiled and thanked them, let them do what they needed to do. I had my solution to this problem, the same way I found the solutions to all my past.

When the cremation ceremony finally came, all I wanted was to carry him on his last journey. I was in uniform and I asked my best mate to be in uniform too. The reason wasn't for my dad, he wasn't military. My uniform shielded me and gave me strength.

After the ceremony I saw my godfather and his son and the anger increased. Hold it together, this wasn't the time. The wake was held at the local pub, everyone toasted him and spilled stories about his life. It was just noise to me because my focus was on someone else.

When I finally got him on his own, he started to spin a story about my Dad. I leaned in to him, pretending I couldn't hear; my inner voice was screaming hit him, take him down, show him your strength, you are no longer a weak child unable to do 100 push-ups. I was imagining where to land my first volley of punches or should I just kick his knee cap out?

I looked across the room, my Grandma was sat looking at me. Her face told me this wasn't the time or the place, I knew that I had to keep control for her sake.

So I looked him in the face and said, "I remember what happened when we were younger, you might not, but I do! Today is your grace, if I ever see you again, I wont be this subdued, you better watch yourself!"

He could see the fire in my eyes, my words had venom and he knew what I meant. With that he finished his drink and decided to leave.

# CHAPTER NINETEEN

# WHEELS FALLING OFF

I stayed off from work for a week, I had to sort a few things out. I was pushing to get things moving, I figured the quicker I could get back to normality the better.

Anything practical I wanted to deal with it as quick as possible. Letters were written to credit card companies; the car was handed back. This wasn't what Dad's wife wanted or needed to do but I did.

I was still angry. How could he run up so much debt? When I checked back, it was obvious though. He was taking cash out of one to pay the other. On the surface he appeared to be a good creditor so the companies kept topping up his limit. Now the ball was in their court; there was nothing in the estate and nobody knew about his debts. We had sought legal advice and they said it should all be written off. Experience had taught me never to rest till you see it in black and white.

When I returned to work, nothing had changed I was still flying hard to gain Combat Ready Status along with plans for winter flying training in Norway. My stress cracks were beginning to show. I was trying to live up to a stupid promise I made to Dad about his wife and deal with his debt along with my normal stuff.

I was taken to one side and it was decided it was probably

best I didn't go to Norway. I was a mix of emotions, work was my only constant, it was for my own good but inside I felt I was letting the team down.

Letters had started to drift back and most credit card companies seemed to be playing ball and writing off his debt. Others needed a second letter; some didn't bother and sent in a debt collection agency. It turned out that even they had a heart and eventually understood that the debts die with someone if there is no estate to claim from.

I was hoping things would now settle down for me. I was still angry, I was turning inwards to try to sort things out, more hours in the gym or on the road, to try and regain a balance with me and my darkness, but every day it seemed heavier, more dense. I had to protect people from both it and from me.

I was engulfing myself in work and thought maybe this could get me back in balance, and again put the darkness away. Flying still gave me the ability to leave my past behind, when that helmet went on it was never about me. I was soon to pass my combat ready check and I wanted more. I wanted to be the best that I could be and I needed a new challenge.

My home life was starting to get turbulent, my wife was feeling that I just wasn't happy. I started to look at our debts for motorbikes, new cars, credit cards, it had to stop, I refused to end like my Dad.

We went back to Yorkshire but only when we had to as this would darken my moods. When we visited Dad's widow, every time we pulled up in the car my stomach would turn. The house hadn't been touched, his glasses, his slippers.

Having to try to keep a promise you hate with every fibre of your body is hard. I was always pleasant, always trying to do things, sort things, but I hated being in the same space as her. She had started to tell the story of the night he died, she was talked through CPR on the telephone and was sponging his sick away from his mouth. I just reassured her, if the heart attack was that big and his kidneys failing there was nothing she could have done. She told the story to everyone who would listen, was it a sympathy thing or was she trying to come to terms with the fact that he died in her arms?

Work knew I was having problems at home. It's amazing what living in married quarters can do. It is a non-stop rumour mill and the rumours soon hit the squadron. Our second Iraq tour was looming, I was looking forward to it, I longed to get away and regain that sense of purpose.

The squadron though thought they were doing me a favour by putting me on standby to go, thus giving me more time at home to try to sort out affairs. They weren't. Standby turned things into a downhill spiral at work, my colleagues were becoming more aware of me not pulling my weight. I was getting banter in the crew room, some harsh, some friendly but it was always based around the same thing. I overheard a couple of people say I was a malinger, a waste of space, a war dodger. I wanted to snap but what was the point?

I just let them think whatever they wanted to. I just took it and held it inside. I was in danger of exploding with all the things I held within.

I only had a few days notice for a job that came up in Iraq, an extra crew was needed so I was off. It was only for six weeks but it was the rest I needed away from my home life, things were too much. The detachment was really uneventful. It consisted mainly of vehicle checks

You flew down a road with two teams, landed on the road, deployed one team to vehicle search, while you stayed in the air, covering and warning them of anything approaching. The second team were there in case a vehicle broke through. It was very mundane, things in Iraq had calmed down in the South, the main problems were still focused in and around Baghdad. Personally, even though it was a bit dull, to me it was fantastic, I was on operations again, my past back in the UK. It also stopped some of the hard times and banter from colleagues, not all of them, to them I was now only half a war dodger as I had only done half the time. I couldn't win, I just let it wash away as at last I was on operations.

Getting back was a problem, I couldn't adjust. Being away was fantastic, it was escapism, why would I want to return? I returned from Iraq to my wife's birthday. Although I had told her I would be back, she still went out with her friends so my first night home was spent alone. I didn't blame her, how could I?

In September my wheels began to come off, I was beginning to lose control, my wife was spending more time away with friends. My Dad's birthday came and went and finally I didn't feel angry towards him. Maybe it was part of the grieving process that the emotions flowed out of me in different ways, not sleeping, not eating, over training. All in all, it was compounded by feeling alone at home.

When the pain of training no longer helped me, I knew things were bad and I needed help. I ended up at the doctors, I explained that I didn't have suicidal thoughts, I just wasn't happy, nothing made me happy anymore. I longed to be on constant operations there I found peace. I was referred to the Department of Community Mental Health (DCMH), the military's specialist head doctors.

I was to meet with a Community Psychiatric Nurse (CPN). When we met, I found I could chat with him about general stuff only, but inside I couldn't connect with him. I didn't have a choice I was assigned him and there was no changing without a very good reason, it is the military way.

The meetings always went the same way. I told him what he wanted to hear. This kept him happy, kept him off my back.

We had had a couple of meetings and the usual came out. I had to go off and every day write my thoughts down in a diary, but his main recommendation was the use of anti-depressants. No way did I want happy pills. If you get on that shit, you will never get off it.

I was doing everything else he asked; writing the diary and not taking caffeine in the afternoon. I had cut out the booze, I was even being sensible in the gym. I knew about the endorphin rush it gave me and didn't train after 7pm, but he kept insisting on the medication. I wasn't strong enough to refuse so, in the end, I took his pills. The one thing he forgot to mention with them was they were one big problem for aircrew, I was no longer allowed to fly or carry live arms.

To make matters worse, the minimum time I was to be on the shit was six months. I spiralled out of control further, my career had hit a wall. I needed to get sorted quickly, I needed to regain my balance and get back to work and a proper training regime without the constant watching eyes.

I don't think he appreciated what he was doing to me, I was feeling low and work was keeping me going. I even was getting a little credibility back from my colleagues as their banter had lessened. I went to work unable to fly again for another six months. People turned against me. Some of it was tongue in cheek, but some was harsh.

The tablets were making me worse, I was lethargic, with no energy. I could train but not to the degree I needed.

I decided to bury myself into work, it wasn't pleasant at home, my wife's shifts were getting longer and more frequent. Her night shift seemed to last weeks, she was working nights and sleeping days; we were ships passing.

My work now was a desk job, I started to sort out the websites and the station's electronic filing system. The military were going through a big change and upgrading systems and operation platforms. I started to get heavily involved not just for my squadron but the entire unit. It was mind numbing, but a welcome distraction. Often I would work late or weekends I had a single office and could close my door, everything seemed easier if I was alone.

Christmas arrived and with it the first anniversary of Dad's death. It's funny how specific days set in your mind. To me he always died Boxing Day, despite the death certificate saying the 27th. I felt it hard and hit the bottle. Combined with the drugs I was on a bad mix, my moods turned black, the darkness had won. I started to consider death, it wasn't the one event but all of them from all my years of pain. No longer could I hide away and control the feelings; the tablets had stopped that by removing my energy. Even in the daylight I was living in darkness.

One bad day, I was weak and I confessed these feelings to my wife, it hurt her badly. Even though she seemed to have disconnected, she still cared at some level; it led to an argument about me being selfish.

So in the New Year I headed back to the doctors after promising my wife I would. I hadn't thought of suicide for days and I needed off the medication as it was causing more harm than good. On confessing this to my doctor, I was locked into the back of a military vehicle, with a medic and a driver, and escorted to DCMH. I was being treated like a psychopath and with this treatment I started to feel a single emotion. The problem was it was anger.

I had a meeting with a psychiatrist. I explained my feelings but thanks to the spark of anger, I was on a level again. I was in control, he didn't try and make things easier. He said to keep taking the tablets; and they might up the dose, that was always the answer, more tablets.

A week later, I took a phone call from my sister; about Grandma who had been taken ill and was in hospital. My sister was shocked I hadn't known. I was straight in the car and headed north; my Grandma meant a lot to me, why hadn't Dad's wife called?

I got to the hospital, I knew she had been ill for some time, but she had tried to hide it from us all as she was so strong. A cancerous growth had pierced her skin and she was dressing the wound on a daily basis by herself. I smiled at her strength, now that is tough. I had some pressing business to sort out; someone was going to get it in the neck for not calling me.

When I left the hospital I headed straight for my Dad's house. "How dare you not phone me about Grandma being in hospital? If Dad was here he would have phoned me straight away!" I bawled at my Dad's wife.

I could sense that the mention of his name hurt her, but it was true. The promise I had made to my father was now broken, from here on she was alone. Seeing my Grandma gave me some strength back, I had to fight, grow strong; these tablets had made me weak. Now it was my time to get back some control and sort this out. I could live with my past providing I had a way of feeling pain or I could escape into work. I had been doing it for nearly 20 years. The tablets had to stop.

I went cold turkey. I stopped there and then, I flushed them away. I knew it would have side effects but only mild as I had only been on them for four months. Sleep was hard but I could live with it, energy was returning to my body and I was soon back to a punishing training routine. I was still working hard at work but now with an extra drive to get back in the air. By getting to grips once again with all the rules and regulations I would prove to people I could hold my own and stop the harsh banter about me being a war dodger. I would show them, make them eat their words.

I only had one task to do to get me in the air and that was to convince a shrink I was mentally fit. I felt fit, I was strong again, I was in control, I had spare capacity, life was coming back into balance and I just needed to keep it that way.

A few days later, I had a review with a shrink at DCMH. I strode into his office, never being a shrinking violet, a good firm handshake and kept eye contact, not too much I didn't want him thinking I was angry, he needed to see control.

I said calmly, "I need to get upgraded, so I can be flying again."

Any talk of my past, I'd planned to counter him and head him off in a different direction. I sat across from him, assessing him and his office. I had noticed some rock albums, albums I had, and there were copies of classic rock next to them. This would be brilliant, my way of steering the conversation if it became uncomfortable.

So the interview started and I let him think he had built a little trust. I would tell him all about my Dad because that's why they had stopped me flying, tell them what they needed to hear. The issue of tablets soon came up, he told me we needed to reduce the dose, it would take a few months.

I was ready for that, "If you check my documents you will find I haven't collected a prescription for any since January, so they must be out of my system."

I was feeling good, I was controlling the interview. He then started with a different set of questions that I wasn't comfortable with. So I used the ace up my sleeve and for the next 10 minutes we were chatting about rock concerts and different bands, fantastic. Eventually, I got the news which was music to my ears. I was to be reinstated and upgraded to full flying duties.

# CHAPTER TWENTY

# THE REFEREE'S COUNTING

I had my balance back and a green light to fly again. I still had a few hoops to jump through and by doing so I would hopefully prove a few points to some people.

I was soon programmed to fly by the squadron. My first flight would be a check flight which was an assessment to see what level I could now fly to. It was with the boss and it was a long one, which covered all aspects. He was so impressed with my performance I was instantly reinstated to combat ready status, despite having over six months off. All that was left to do was to show my doubting colleagues, I was back in full flow and I pulled my weight.

I volunteered for everything going, anything short notice I was at the top of the list. I even volunteered to help our opposite squadron with detachments in Italy and policing the G8 summit in Scotland, I did anything to get on with the job and keep my balance.

When I came back from Iraq last year, there was an atmosphere between my wife and I. Something didn't feel right and with all my volunteering she was getting sick of my post it notes on the fridge 'I'm going away with work. I don't know when I'll be home. I will phone if I can.'

I returned from the G8 summit, I hadn't been home a day and she told me, she wanted to move out, she was leaving me. My heart sank, I couldn't believe my ears, "You want to do what?"

She repeated herself "I want to move out, it's not working."

Just as I thought my life was back in balance, it was about to be thrown out again. I was searching for anything to hold onto, I couldn't have this happen to me now, not now. We chatted but it ended in an argument, I couldn't stand it, feelings were rushing around inside me, what should I do?

I knew what the answer was, I got my runners, I knew it was coming, I had to, I had to push. My stomach was churning from what she had just told me, I had to run and get those feelings away and get that good feeling back into my head. So I found a hill and did sprint reps until I was sick, now I was ready to sort this out.

I moved into the spare room, this way she agreed to stay. I had to fight to keep her just to keep my balance. Over the next couple of weeks I tried everything. I booked Relate counselling, she refused to go. I was prepared to do anything to keep her, granted it was for selfish and wrong reasons, it wasn't for love.

Every night was the same, I would lay awake in the spare room with my wife next door. I would be searching for answers and her phone would be constantly bleeping with incoming text messages, she was holding conversations with someone late into the night. It got too much, I was keeping too much inside, I was going to explode.

I knew she seeing someone else so I confronted her but she never admitted it, I had to get some balance back and keep the darkness from totally consuming me so she had to leave. The torture from hearing her phone had to stop, she was already adding insult to injury.

So before another argument started I blurted it out,

"Get the fuck out of the house, if you want to leave you are moving out!"

I could have phrased it better but I was past the stage of caring. The very next day, still raw, we discussed our futures, we wanted a quick divorce. I just wanted her away, she could have the lot, house, furniture everything, providing I could get to the gym and stay in the air. Material objects meant nothing to me; they were just reminders of the past.

I told them at work she was moving out, it's not uncommon for servicemen to have a divorce or two under their belt. It wasn't that she was leaving that was troubling me, it was I had failed at a marriage. I next did the worst thing possible by hitting the bottle, the military's answer to most problems. Nothing mattered any more, the booze helped me sleep, the hangovers made me train harder.

I gave her what furniture she wanted, I even helped her move out. It all seemed a little too easy for her. When she was gone, I pulled down the garage door and I was left with a TV and a sofa, an old bed, and a chest of drawers, but I didn't care. I went to the fridge, a Jack Daniels and dry was needed.

I had just settled down to a conversation with Jack when the door bell chimed. It was my neighbour, he had seen what was happening. He said he was sorry, he couldn't get involved, but he then told me about a 4x4 which pulled up on a night and left early, every time I was out of the way with work practically. It had been there every day while away policing the G8 summit and before that when I was away in Iraq.

It all became clear this last year had been a joke, they both must have been laughing at me, but I was going to have the last laugh. Thoughts of revenge ravaged my brain and I put both of them on quite a long list of people who had hurt me and I wanted to get even with.

I couldn't do it though, what would be the point? I prefer to take the pain, that's what good people do. That's what knights in armour do, I was a protector, I protected people from pain.

After the neighbour's visit, other people confirmed his story, I thanked them all, now it was time to sort things out. I had many debts from the marriage with new cars, fancy holidays and diamonds. It was solicitor time, I didn't have the energy for any more fights, she looked over everything and stopped me from giving it all away. My wife could have some of the debt too, that'd stop her laughter. As long as I was debt free and I could start again, I could walk away with my head held high. I was tired of fighting the last 20 years, this had been the final straw, now my head was full of darkness. I had hit the canvas and the referee was counting me out.

I started to think about things, in a darker way than ever before, I was tired, it was everything, constant dark thoughts popped in and out. They just kept getting more extreme, one minute I would be driving down the road, hoping for a car to pull out and wipe me out. In busy places, I walked around bumping into people, trying to antagonise one brave bastard to start something, so I had an excuse to fight.

The nights were always plagued by nightmares keeping me awake. The more I tried to fight it, the slower the referee's count became. There was only one way to deal with this tiredness and stop the darkness. It was to find the ultimate way out, it was time to end everything, to end me.

My good side tried to find a daily reason to stay alive; it only needed one, to keep me going, to keep me fighting. It was too late though as a darker thought had surfaced; for my light to be extinguished. There was only one answer, suicide.

# Chapter Twenty-one

# LONG AND WINDING ROAD

As I came round I checked the time, we had been sat there for over two hours.

The homeopath had been making notes all that time, it was disjointed, I was flitting from one story to the next. All of them factual, no emotions were present, I didn't know her so I wasn't that comfortable with showing her how vulnerable and weak I had become. The raw stories from the past few years gave her a glimpse of how deep and dark things had become. My deep childhood stories I was yet to share with her, this wasn't the right time for me.

I had to trust her like I had trusted no one else. No matter what came out, she sat there, no judgement. Only understanding and warmth flowed from her, warmth I hadn't felt at any time in my past. It was now her turn, she sat and chatted about a way forward.

As she spoke, she did research on her MacBook, she turned it around. What I read were the emotions and feelings I had being describing, right there on her screen. She stood up, while I continued to read, I couldn't quite believe how true it scanned. She went across to the pill bottles, removed one and began to make me a remedy.

She was concerned about my darkness so, we set about trying to lighten it. She explained sometimes they worked just a little but when you got the right one, it would be like taking the sucker punch. You hit the canvas and there will be no getting up. Your body will get what it needs, time to rest and heal itself, it was a question of finding the right one.

It was my turn to ask some questions like could I take them without side effects and were they legal. I was always tested by the military drugs test team. I was worried about my career, I didn't have the energy to fight an investigation. She reassured me.

My brain settled, my head was a little fuzzy and then an overwhelming sense of tiredness hit me. I was aware of how much time I had taken and offered her extra money but she refused.

She showed me to the door after we had made another appointment for a week later. She told me to call if I felt my darkness was too much for me to fight alone. I got into my car, everything was shaking. I had to get home.

I pushed the start button and headed down the winding rode, I made it to the car park the one from where I had recce'd the place some hours earlier, I didn't care any longer about the curtain twitches, I pulled into car park and my dam burst. Tears rolled down my cheeks, I wasn't thinking about any one event it was them all coming out. I sat for what seemed like an hour until I could control myself.

When I regained control, I realised I may have found some answers to my darkness, and an ally to help me find some answers and help me with my fight. I got home and I wanted to sleep. I was so tired I could sleep for a week but I had to go to work the next day. That was tomorrow, today I started to release some darkness. I decided the only way she could truly help, was if she knew about all my demons, about what made the darkness truly black. Over the next few sessions, she would be told about everything, no stone would be left unturned.

When I eventually told her everything, she realised how dark things had become for me and she set about getting me back on the right path. With her belief in me, I decided it was time to tell someone else too, the doctor at the unit. He wasn't surprised and he took it well.

After he then said it "I'm sorry but we need to get you some proper help with stuff like that, not just a homeopath."

I thought he was going back on his word to send me to our military head doctors as that would mean no more flying and a return to the tablets. My career would be over and with it me. I started to shake, he then reassured me that we would seek someone privately. He had friends who could help and he wouldn't send me to the military ones.

So the next time I visited him, he had big news, he had found me someone in London, highly recommended by a friend. His department's budget would even go and pick up the bill, he had kept his word and finally I was going to be sorted out forever.

Getting to know a new therapist takes time as they only have you for an hour at a time. I was lucky with my homeopath to be able to bond so quickly. When I went to London for the first time, even though I was comfortable because I trusted my doctor, the therapist was a little hippy-like for me. But I owed my doctor the same trust he had shown me, I would give her a fair go.

The therapy started, the appointments seemed to come in chunks, we would work on different aspects of my life and then take a month off. This was because she had clinics world wide. With every chunk of appointments, backed up with homeopathy every 2-3 weeks, things were coming together. I was beginning to understand my past and it was time to start dealing with it.

In London, we dealt in a very practical way with the abuse. I was to sit in a coffee shop and check out every bloke in there, and the ones passing the windows, to see if I was attracted to any of them. It was a strange thing to do, but it was making a difference, I was getting better. With the experience from the coffee shop we established I wasn't interested in the same sex. We then would move onto the next issue.

We role played about family situations and different scenarios from my past; building my confidence, so I could go and do it for real. The one thing she never truly grasped though was my issues with work. The accident with my knee, the personalities and the alleged child porn. I had stopped thinking of revenge a long time ago, it was easier to bury it to some level.

With war itself, she had some experience. She'd helped many troubled servicemen and veterans. Iraq to me seemed so insignificant and even she realised it was my way of escaping and she was happy I had dealt with it on my own. I was ready to move on, but first I had to deal with the source of my darkness from the past; I needed to go back to Yorkshire and face some people.

I returned from London on the train, I phoned my boss and asked him for the next few days off. I was heading back, to where the darkness began. I had an agenda planned out in my head and I wasn't changing it for anybody. First was my Dad's wife, then Grandma and then Mum.

I walked into my Dad's old bungalow; she was still in the same place and still hadn't moved on. I went in and she was shocked to see me, this wasn't a time for small talk. Get in, get out, keep control, its pointless pulling punches.

"I have decided I don't want you in my life any more. You were my Dad's wife, we have history it is pointless denying it but I need to move into the future, without my past and you are not invited along with me."

I went on without letting her get a word in. "If I ever see you at my Grandma's I will be polite and things, but as regards any other connections between us they end now."

She was understandably shocked, but tried getting a little control of the situation. She said OK and started with a speech that I didn't owe her so I turned and walked. I closed the door, job done, I would never return.

When I got to my car a different emotion came over me, that of relief. The next visit was going to be the hardest, I owed my Grandma a full explanation, her house was two minutes away. I had to keep going.

I sat with her for about an hour. Several cups of tea later and she understood that it was my choice. I wasn't doing it out of maliciousness. I told her I had forgiven people from my past and there was no place for them in my future. I left Grandma in no uncertainty that I would always be there for her.

It was then time for my Mum. I had pre-warned her the night before I was coming and she had to be alone, if she respected me she would be. I stood at the top of the drive and I could see her in the living room. I knew the thing was not to feel guilty about my decision or explain how I felt. Just say my piece, let her know I am doing OK and move on. Don't let her turn it around.

I tapped on the patio doors, I didn't feel comfortable just walking in, not now. She smiled, opened the door and tried to hug me. I wasn't ready to hug her. I wasn't there for a reconciliation; I wasn't there for her; I was here for me. With yet another coffee, we sat on the patio, I explained things were going OK for me, that the divorce was settled and I was waiting for a new apartment to be built. To soften the blow I was about to deliver, I told her I had been awarded a commendation by the service.

I then shifted the conversation to explain why I had not been in contact for the last nine months. I explained I wasn't ready for any family in my life, not yet. I still needed to sort things out. I told her I had just cut my Dad's wife out of my life for ever and if she didn't want the same thing to happen between us, I needed time and space. When I was ready, at some point in the future I would like to be a part of the family again.

This was not to be all of them mind as my stepbrother had become a liability and had inherited some of his Dad's bad side if he had a drink in him. He would lose control and I didn't like it, he was always trying to provoke me, I didn't need it or like it. He reminded me of his Dad and the wicked things he did to my family. My only wish is he will keep control and never put his own family through it. She seemed to understand but then, behind me, the gate opened and my sister arrived unexpectedly. I hadn't planned for this.

I stood up, looked at her and blurted, "I'm off, take care."

I passed my sister on the path, we exchanged pleasantries, I said I was leaving, it wasn't because she had arrived and that I'd see her around. I didn't have bad feelings towards my sister.

I was still protecting them from me but they probably couldn't see it. I got to my car, it had been a draining morning, I needed some therapy. It was off to my old friend's gym and a good hard training session. I headed for my safe place and a warm smile, a good coffee, great conversation, just what the doctor ordered.

When I returned to therapy in London and to my homeopath, I told them all about my visit and the subsequent fallout; aunties and uncles telling me I couldn't choose my family without Dad's wife. I'd ended up losing them too but that was their decision. I needed to do what was right for me and this was it.

My homeopath and I worked together for the next few weeks and, in the end, I was told I was ready, that things had been sorted, my darkness appeared to have gone. I kept telling myself I had forgiven everyone from my past and I believed myself to some level. Emotionally I felt nothing could harm me ever again. I was stronger than ever, my past was my past.

I now had two people I could call to help me if I needed them. I arranged with my homeopath I would try and go back every year for my personal 'MOT' and a catch up.

It was time to dismount from my horse and stop being everyone's knight in armour. I had some battle scars but now I had taken off my armour and beaten it back in to shape. With it removed, I could finally heal some of the wounds on the inside too.

Once healed, I knew I could get back on my horse and continue riding through life's journey. I will keep my armour to one side but I hope I never have to wear it again.

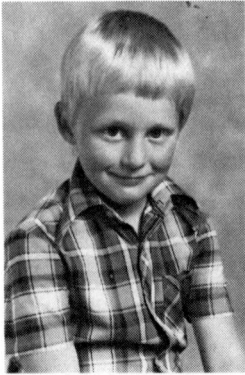

Innocent

**From a teenager Matt hated photographs because who he saw in the pictures, he hated the most.**

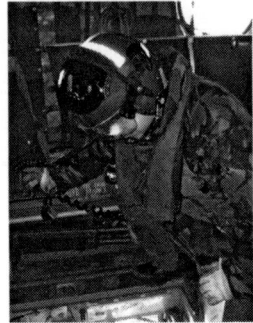

Checking a load
beneath the Chinook

Iraq
Waiting for the Call to Go.

Iraq
Tired out after a Mission

Will it open ?

**Some People find time for pictures — There was no time in Afganistan.**

Checking underneath before landing in the mountains

Run away — Complete Bike Therapy Lands End to John 'o' Grotes

Another Award

All Better and Working with Team Talking2Minds!

Sport was the only way I could feel alive

# Chapter Twenty two

# Staying Grey

As I sat on the RAF Tristar flying to Afghanistan, I was feeling pretty lonely. It was good to have time before operations to try to work out why things were happening. The darkness had gone. All I wanted was happiness now but why did I feel like people were trying to drag me down and hold me back?

It had been a while since I'd been away with work and they weren't letting me forget it. This wasn't helping how I felt about the whole situation. For the last six months, I hadn't felt a part of the squadron. My only hope was that in the field I could prove myself and show them all once again that I was a part of the team. And not just any part of the team but someone who is professional, reliable and great at his job.

Last year I'd had issues, not dark ones, but my knee finally gave way on the interrogation survival course on Dartmoor. It was one of those things, since the aircraft incident of 2001 I had been protecting it, always aware of it's limitation and only pushing the limits when I had no choice. The uneven ground, finally broke it, so I'd had an operation and months of rehab, I couldn't join the guys on their first summer deployment to Afghanistan. It was a hard tour for them, a rack of bravery medals and honours were awarded. They did fantastically well but, most importantly, they all came back.

The squadron were ready for the off again in October, this time to Morocco. Despite my knee not being ready, I had to go. People were at me yet again with snippy comments about my time off and not going away. If they only they knew what hell I had lived through and how I lived for deployment as my respite from the darkness. I didn't want them to know this but I did need their approval and acceptance as a part of the team.

I nursed my knee through the detachment and as soon as I hit the soil in the UK, I was back in rehab to strengthen my knee, I was on the treadmill and my ankle turned. Lucky for me, the remedial instructor was there. I hobbled back into the squadron, for a while they had thought I had snapped my ankle. It started again, I got it both barrels from the second-in-command of the squadron, someone I trusted as a friend. I knew there was a rank structure but the way he went about it meant there was something more, it was payback.

I got a big lecture about how I injured myself and how I was untrustworthy. He tore strips off me, everything was questioned. I stood and just had to look through him, I could feel it again, sharp. It was returning, not the darkness but the anger. He kept it coming and it was a verbal onslaught. When the knife was fully in, he then twisted it, "We cannot trust you to go to Afghanistan!"

That took the wind right out of me. I was getting a hard time from some people anyway without that bombshell. He'd won this fight but not the battle, I vowed to show him and show them all.

Over the next weeks I got down to some serious rehab for both knee and ankle and, after three weeks, I was back in the air. My first test was to pass an external examiner's check. I passed with flying colours. That should keep them off my back, maybe I could go to Afghanistan now?

I headed to my boss to see, but the answer was still no, what was I supposed to do? The anger of the last few weeks was disappearing, a new emotion took its place, that of disappointment. I vowed again just keep my head up and to keep going, not to let the pack mentality bring me down, not again. All I wanted in life was to be happy, with no more darkness.

Over Christmas, I decided it was time to try and get to know my Mum and her husband again. I extended an olive branch as they had respected my privacy and I felt it was time to try and see if we could be a family again. Things went well, I didn't feel guilty, it was pleasant and it seemed to work. With this new positive version of me, I returned to work in the right frame of mind. The guys were off in a month so they had lots of flying, simulators, tactics and new weapon systems to sort. I had nothing planned I still wasn't going as I couldn't yet be trusted!

It's not in my nature to sit back and mope, so I thought I'd be constructive to maybe help someone who was going. I called my crewman leader and asked him, "What shall I do, while you guys are in Scotland? Is there anything you need sorting for Afghanistan?"

He looks at me puzzled, "What do you mean?"

I'd been told I'm not going away and they'd kept him out of the loop but he is meant to be my reporting point. What great management skills. I explained the whole story, he could see it in my face. I am feeling it, the loneliness, being apart from the rest of our team. Ten minutes later, I was called to the office, I'm off with them to Scotland to help with their pre-deployment training. This was sort of good news. I just had to fit in around others as I was still not going away and low priority. I'd be as professional as ever, I could go and tell them to screw it, but I wouldn't, I didn't want any more conflict. I thought it may help bring some of my doubters back onto my side. In the end though, Scotland ended up being a waste of time.

It was pointless making an issue of it as the week after I was going on the interrogation survival course again and I needed to focus all my attention there. The survival course consists of two weeks on and near Dartmoor, learning different skills, evading the enemy and then being captured and interrogated twice. There is no way of escaping it. It has been designed that way, everyone gets captured. I found it easy to detach, orange boiler suits donned, no buttons; it is going to get cold; it is all a part of the softening up process.

Some of the stress positions they hold you in are very uncomfortable, but when you have lived with my darkness of the past, being interrogated isn't a problem. I know how to control what's inside; don't antagonise them, stay grey; make it look like you are giving them what they want. It was an interesting 24 hours.

Week two they give you tools to help you resist the interrogators. I just listened on, the relaxation and the grey stuff it wasn't new to me. Then it is back to being interrogated, more softening stress positions and more interrogation, for a further 24 hours. At the end, we are asked how real we found it. It did feel real enough to know you don't want to be captured. It was a massive hurdle for me to clear, after last year's failure with my knee giving in. The level of interrogation training needed depends on who you are or what job you do, this was one of the top levels. I was so glad I'd done it. It was an experience and inside it is great to know I can keep self control even when antagonised. I just wondered if now I am trusted enough to go to Afghanistan.

It was almost comical when I returned to the squadron as two crewman had gone on the interrogation course. Rumours had hit the streets saying one had failed, everyone instantly assumed it was me. I don't fail, failure isn't something I do well or at all, if I'm physically able to do it, I will.

The crewman leader stopped me on my way in, he was smiling, "Great news you passed, I have got you on the detachment and you are coming with us to Afghanistan ..."

I smiled, fantastic I was going, I needed to get stuff sorted; my brain went into operations mode, some brain cells which hadn't been used since Iraq.

I was soon brought down to earth when I heard him say, "... but only for half the detachment."

My heart sank, half! I needed and wanted the full time there. My brain raced off again with a new idea, I would get all my kit and ground training sorted and maybe, just maybe I'd get a chance to go with them at the start. I had to get things sorted out, kitting, medical and I needed to learn the new mini-gun weapon system. I needed help, I would have to call in a few old favours. My colleagues were off in four days, I had a preliminary date in March, a whole month after the guys.

A month is too long I thought, I would be ready in days. Along with deployment away there is a lot of box ticking to do before you are officially ready to go. I had managed to negotiate everything to be completed for the end of the following week. I would be missing some equipment, but I would overcome that. My tactical knowledge wasn't up to scratch like the others as I had missed the flying both in the aircraft and simulators, being low priority. I had loads of experience from my past though and I would study to get on top of things.

I had to get the mini-gun sorted, I needed that

knowledge, it was going to defend us. I had to ask a big favour from a friend to get some one to one tuition. The live firing day and night checks would have to wait as they couldn't fly a special sortie just to qualify me. I did what I do best and found a way to adapt and overcome. There are no problems, just solutions, nothing was going to stop me this time. I am no war dodger!

The next week was full of regiment ground training; standard stuff, weapons, first aid, ground tactics, improvised explosive devices. For me, it was starting with a long range shoot. I so enjoyed getting some rounds down, it was all very calming, until my phone went; a message had come in from Afghanistan, one of the crewman was injured. Already?

"Could I be ready for Friday or Saturday?"

I was stunned, excited and happy and answered with a definite yes. This was my chance, I had to get some things sorted. The week was going to be very busy and within a few days, all my boxes were ticked.

I called into the squadron for my final notice to deploy, people appeared to be taken aback, I think they were expecting me not be ready, but I was ready, in a very short space of time. I was on a high, excited about going, yet a little apprehensive. Afghanistan was proving to be a volatile operation. You had to take your 'A-Game' over there as there is no place for anything else.

Despite having everything sorted, it was time to pin my ears back for another talking to from the second-in-command. It was all about the guys out there and I had to prove myself to them. He didn't want me to regress into my dark days. He suggested working at 80% capacity so I didn't burn out and let people down again and not using the gym as I might get injured. I didn't think he wanted me or trusted me to go. I had jumped through all the hoops and got my shit sorted out, why shouldn't I go?

I wasn't going to let him bring me down. I decided to go and see a close friend, he had done his share of ops. I needed to get a good kit check, we stripped out everything, checked, and rechecked, I had what I needed. If you do get shot down and had to move, all you really needed was ammo, water, weapon stripping kit, maybe a couple of dried rations and more ammo.

The night before, one last chance, unpack, repack, double and triple check. I wasn't going to let myself down. I was ready, I finally felt tired the last couple of weeks had been hectic; I hadn't had a real chance to take stock of what was going on, I was feeling tired and I needed sleep.

My alarm buzzed at 5.45am; time to get up and get sorted. The excitement of operations had returned. Get the house locked down, turn the central heating on to holiday mode, unplug everything. It was 6.20am before I knew it, 15 minutes and I needed out. Just time for one last decent brew. It felt weird wearing desert camouflage again. With my bergan loaded and on my back, holdall of extra kit in hand, I was off. Today was going to be long day as a full extra crew were leaving on the same flight. A couple of the guys had their doubts about me but it wasn't the time or place for that. We had to all get on, personnel feelings about each other shouldn't come into it when you are on operations.

The coach arrived. Destination RAF Brize Norton for the Tristar to Kandahar, Afghanistan. The others were making last minute phone calls to loved ones and friends. I just smiled, I was off again, and settled into my seat with my iPod playing in my ears.

This time was different as there was no past to leave behind.

# CHAPTER TWENTY THREE

# INCOMING

The Tristar wheels touched down with a bump. Just to let you know you are arriving into a war zone, on the approach you are required to put on body armour and a helmet. This is to protect you from small arms fire on the final approach. Even in the dead of night someone may get a lucky shot off in your direction and we are in an airliner.

It was around 4am local time, this place is 3½ hrs ahead of the UK, the flight had taken just over seven hours. With the usual faff, it took a little while to disembark.

I was back in operations mode, no time for thinking about anything else, I had to prove myself. You are immediately hit with the arid smell typical of the Middle East. It doesn't matter which part you go to, it all smells the same and it's not pleasant. The place was wet as it was the rainy season and the dust turns to mush so you get filthy. We weren't here to be inspected though, there was a job to be done.

We all followed like sheep to a tent on an airfield. As we walked in, two of our guys were there to meet us. I got another reminder from the newly promoted crewman leader, "Hello mate, I had to fight to get you out here. Don't let me down."

Bloody typical. My feet had just touched the ground

and I was already being observed. The guys spun out their stories about the last few days. There was no real pant splitting excitement, but to me this was new and I was determined to find my feet quick. I had worked alongside the crewman leader before in Iraq and he was quick to reassure me it was like Iraq except it had a few hills and that the base in Kandahar was run by the Americans so was pretty comfortable . After the usual welcome brief - paperwork, sign for your weapon, find your baggage from the mountain of bergans and foot lockers. It was then time to get to our digs and get our heads down for a bit.

The accommodation is pretty good. Courtesy of our good American friends we had metal hard built blocks, aircon, good showers and toilets. Much better than our Brit built stuff. I was impressed. The room had five bunks, a few guys had rolled through here before us and had started to make it user friendly, leaving foldaway chairs, fabric foot lockers by the beds and the weave of para cord across the room to hang things from.

If I had any nerves, they had left me as it was feeling like Iraq. It certainly smelt like it and, even though it wasn't a tent, the insides were the same. Just as we turned in for a few hours' kip, the range started to fire up. Some guys were getting some lead down, probably zeroing their weapon in readiness for their tour. I never had a problem sleeping on ops, maybe my brain goes into a different mode, even in my dark days I always could sleep.

In no time at all the lights were on, it was lunch time and an opportunity to take a look at the place in the light of day. We drove around in our Land Rovers, the American presence was high, but other nations were here too - Canadians, Dutch and a few Australians. In the middle of the base, stood a wooden square, known locally as the 'Boardwalk'. One thing the Americans do like are their creature comforts.

Around the outside of the Boardwalk were fast food joints, a Canadian Timmy Horton's coffee shop and souvenir shops and on the inside basketball, roller hockey and seats where you could eat your junk food.

It was time to get to work and start sorting out my flying kit and climbing the 'Everest' mountain of rules and regulations. This involved starting to familiarise myself with the new equipment and the layout on board the Chinook. Things were real. If you had any doubts you are on operations when you get your pistol, choice of how much ammo, smoke grenades and morphine, you have a wake up call. I stopped thinking about people observing me, I was here to do a job and I would do it to the best of my abilities. I wouldn't let anyone or myself down.

The day had gone quickly. At the end of the day, a mate decided to come for a stroll with me so we could chew the fat before going to the mess hall for dinner. He was a pal, not one of the doubters. I was picking his brains, wanting any top tips, the usual stuff, I was wanting to be on the top of my game and quick. On the way there, we heard it, a sound I last heard in Iraq and once heard, never forgot, whoosh, then you wait, you know its coming.

BANG!!

The base had just had an incoming rocket; the guys had been here for over a week and nothing. I'm here a day and bang. The sirens started, we looked at each other, no body armour, no helmet. We just shrugged, oh well best we head back to the accommodation. On the way back, there were people running into the nearest shelter. It didn't phase us, just head back to the rooms and keep out of the way, it's too late when you hear the bang. The bad guys had got their ranging right, the rocket hit inside the camp. I didn't know if there were any injuries but was sure we would find out in the next couple of days.

There were no further rockets that night. The next morning nothing was said about casualties or where it had landed, just another day on ops. Today's tasks were getting briefings from different people about the Taliban and their weapon capabilities. It was now up to me, I needed to keep at it, I felt I had so much to learn and not a lot of time to do it. So as boring as it was, I had my nose to the books, code words, evasion plans. Many things had changed since I was last in Iraq. Then there was the political crap, you have to have the right driving licence, the right pass for getting onto the airfield despite being aircrew. When bases become established the admin bullshit soon follows. This place was no different. Why can't people accept we are living in a shit hole and all we really want to do is go home and let them have their shit hole back? Why do narrow minded people make things harder than they need to be?

I started to feel ready and I needed to be because tomorrow I was programmed for a full days flying. My first look at the notorious Helmand Province.

# CHAPTER TWENTY-FOUR

# A BAPTISM OF FIRE

The mission brief started at 7.45am, we already had been there an hour preparing the aircraft and our kit for the day. The day's flying was a set of several different mini-missions. First take people, supplies and post to various forward operating bases (FOBs) before heading to our UK main hub, Camp Bastian. Then shut down our aircraft, refuel and then go into another mission brief for the second half of the day.

I was feeling a nervous excitement, my crewman buddy was the crewman leader. He was an old hand with years of experience; he was going to instruct me over the next few days and get me going. When we turned up at the aircraft there were a lot of people and kit.

With the aircraft fully loaded, it was time for the off. My job is to pull up the rear ramp as today I'm down the back, getting people and kit on and off. It also meant doing regular engineering scan checks and manning the rear M60 weapon, but most important was my look out quadrant. We are constantly checking for any incoming fire or other aircraft, so we all have specific areas to check depending on where we are in the aircraft. The area is split into an imaginary clock face, today my quadrant is from the 6 o'clock to the 10 o'clock position.

The flight up to Bastian was uneventful. I saw some of the FOBs and started to get a feel for the lay of the land. Some of the bases were in towns and there are always spying eyes on the ground observing or 'dicking you' on your way in. It was their way of trying to spot any chinks in our armour. Did we have the same routine? What were we bringing in and did we make a quick opportunist target?

When the wheels hit the dirt, you want everyone off and on quick. The Taliban would love to take down a Chinook; it is high on their shopping list. The rumour is they have a price list ranging from killing a ground troop, blowing up a vehicle, taking down an aircraft and taking out a base. The higher the target they take out, the more dollars they receive for their efforts.

It was nice to get the first few hours out of the way. Nothing dramatic happened, however this is no place to get complacent. Everyone out here knows this place can hurt you in the blink of an eye. It was my first time at Camp Bastian so another set of base procedures to learn. We held two Chinooks here and they are always ready to go. One is for Immediate Response Tasking (IRT) where we have to be in the air within 15 minutes during the day or 30 minutes at night. The second aircraft is used for High Response Flights (HRF), if someone needs a quick resupply or a mission needs extra aircraft we are ready to go within an hour or less.

It is Tent City here, not like the American base; it is easy to spot our tent as there is a big Day Glow sign on top of it. My turn for shift here was the next week so it was best I just absorb what I could from our flying visit today.

The operations tent was buzzing with a lot of people for another mission briefing. This mission would use three Chinooks and two Apaches to re-supply one of the FOBs. We have a specific briefing format designed for everyone to learn what is going on and what is expected from your aircraft, along with up to date intelligence reports.

Today's mission is for two Chinook aircraft with underslung loads, ours is a big pile of ammo. The third Chinook is full of troops and we have the two Apaches to cover our arses if needed. Next came all the communication procedures and evasion plan. It doesn't matter what rank or crew position, anyone can ask questions at briefs as everyone needs to be singing off the same song sheet.

We already have a slight problem. One of our radio is on the blink so we will have to use good old code words for everything. This isn't too much of a problem.

When we get to our aircraft, a feeling of excitement is flowing through me. This is more like it, we're off to a different part of the country, the Kajaki Dam to the North-east which is one of the two major hydroelectric plants powering Helmand. Tactically we have a base there and it keeps taking some incoming from the Taliban wanting to disrupt operations. It was time to prepare myself mentally, run through my drills, underslung load safety, rules of engagement, the code words, everything was clear in my head. We soon had our aircraft up and running, then the usual Chinook faff began. One of the Chinooks broke down, so we re-planned everything to go on the two left, then a call from ops, the mission is on hold to see if we can go as planned with all three.

Then the second Chinook suddenly developed a problem, so that left us with the only one serviceable Chinook. Another call from ops this time to shut down the aircraft and wait; we cut the engines, stopped the rotors but remained on board waiting for further developments. The radio crackled, we would be going with two Chinooks, our engineers had managed to get one working, and the two

Apaches. We were soon rotors turning and airborne, off to where our load of ammo was waiting.

The third aircraft sprang back into life, we are now back to the original plan, three Chinooks and two Apaches. You have to be flexible to fly, this always happens. The aircraft are continually developing minor or major problems as this is a harsh environment for mechanical things. The 'old birds' take a pounding from the weather or the sheer amount of flying hours, never mind the weight they have to carry on a daily basis.

This is a different part of Afghanistan; the rest of the crew kept calling specific check features so I could start to orientate myself with the terrain and in which direction there would be relative safety. At 3000-4000 feet it is only the big features you really rely on. The area was mix of densely populated places, farms, poppy fields and then areas of nothing, followed by some foothills leading to mountains. My job now is load safety. I have to monitor it along with keeping watch on my quadrant which is back and to the left, from around the 6 o'clock position all the way around to the 10 o'clock position.

The problem with flying things underneath an aircraft is how they fly. We have a special trials unit who test everything and give you limits. Every load is different, it can depend on who constructed it on the ground. Today's was flying well, it is heavier than advertised but they always are. This doesn't help us with calculating fuel and speed but it can also lead to problems with how quickly we can descend, climb and turn. If, at any time, the load is dangerous or is going to impede us getting away from a sticky situation, the captain or I could, if necessary, jettison it. This pile of ammo would cause a big smoking hole in the ground if it came to that.

It was a slow long transit but finally the dam came in sight. We were all beginning to get ready for the drop off just to the edge of dam. We started to slowly take off our height down in a safe area.

One Apache was covering us and one had gone ahead. We were to be the last aircraft to go in. One Chinook was already dropping its load into one landing site. The second had the troops to drop off at a landing site overlooking the dam; we were setting up for our run in when our missile warning alarms sounded.

We have different systems to detect various scenarios and some of them initiate an automatic flare response. Ours had been triggered so my training took over and I started scanning. My quadrant is over the water so unless the Taliban had submarines it wasn't this direction.

"Back left clear" I called.

Others were checking in, the radio buzzed into life it was the Apache escort, the landing site was hot. He had been telling us on the radio but he had forgotten ours was on the blink. The alarm sounded again, the pilot pulled some power in and initiated a climb, it was time to get away. One Chinook was on the ground, guys half in and half out, the other had dropped its load and rapidly got out. We pulled steady power and flew away, scanning to see if we were taking fire. The load was looking OK, no need to jettison it. Everyone was happy and we were sure we hadn't taken rounds. The consensus from the front of the aircraft was that the missile system probably initiated because someone was taking a few shots at us with the Taliban weapon of choice, the good old AK-47.

Welcome to Afghanistan, you just accept it, there is nothing you can do. Everyone was OK, everything was working and we kept the ammo. Now we were back at a safe height, with one Chinook in front and an Apache escort in our 9 o'clock a few hundred meters away, keeping an eye on us both. The guys in the front Chinook buzzed over the radio, their underslung load had also been heavier than advertised, they couldn't get much further, they were flying on fumes and needed to divert for some gas; they were happy to go alone. The Apache was ours, we were heading home to Camp Bastian, mission incomplete.

The Apache was on our left hand side, in my lookout arc. He was moving between the 8 and 9 o'clock position still within a few hundred meters, at between 3000 and 4000 feet, no small arms or rocket propelled grenades (RPG) could reach this height, the radios were quiet and we were heading for home.

The missile alarm warning system rang out, firing a volley of flares. What was it this time another false alarm? Best I get my eyes out and check my quadrant.

As I scanned out of the window, I noticed our Apache escort had also fired some flares; I called it over the intercom, wondering if ours going off had caused his to fire as he was pretty close in. I had to keep scanning, behind and all the way to the 10 or 11 o'clock positions, what could have set it off? I was sweeping with my eyes and moving my head. I was in the 9 o'clock, our system had automatically fired off a second volley of flares and then I saw it, a spiralling grey smoke, just outside our rotor disc.

What the hell?

My brain was buzzing with a shopping list of Taliban weapons; 7.62mm no, RPG no, mortars no, the spiral was moving towards the front fired flare. A loud bang rang out and a pressure wave passed through me. It felt like my fillings were rattling loose. This was something I had never felt before.

Were we hit? What the hell was that?

The bang rang out in my ears, the pressure wave made my entire body uneasy. Finally a light bulb moment for me, I was about to speak when the co-pilot came on the intercom.

When he saw it taking the second forward firing flare he knew what it was, I too had realised what was happening. It was a surface to air missile (SAM).

The spiralling grey smoke; I followed it with my eyes and saw it explode, it was away from us now, but it got close, too close for anybody's comfort. My body was still experiencing the pressure wave of it. There was a second's silence, before we all jumped back into the moment and the training took over.

The pilots were jabbering on the radio, "Contact wait out."

The load was stable; my arse was needed on the ramp so I could have a really good look behind us, could I work out the firing point? I looked in the 6 o'clock position scanning, were the hell had it come from?

Was there a second one coming at us? Not that you can see a missile at cruising speed, but it's smoke trail is the tell tale sign.

Scan. Scan. Where was it?

I couldn't find the firing point and there didn't appear to be a second one in the air. I called it over the intercom, best to reassure the guys we were all doing our jobs. The pilots were compiling a shot report to send to the HQ, now it was time to check on the bang.

I'd had a cursory glance on the way to the ramp, I needed a detailed inspection and I wanted the guys at the front to do the same but they had other tasks first. The shot report, a warning to anyone else in the area to avoid the place. I signalled the other crewman to keep an eye on the load, I was checking everything, the engines, the gear boxes. What was that bang?

Everything appeared normal; we hadn't taken damage; the radios had cooled off. I reassured the guys everything my end was fine; it was a nudge for them to check theirs'.

We discussed the event, although it was only a few minutes ago. It felt like a different day, the bravado started, very few aircrew had come that close. Inside I still wasn't settled, the bang and the pressure wave were immense. The pilots said it was the sonic boom of the missile because it had got that close us, but why had it got that close?

Our equipment had worked in the final second or so. No way should have it got this near. The chatting ended as we all started to reflect in our own heads about what had just happened. The Chinook had a few different missile detection systems and thankfully today they worked.

We were back at Camp Bastian; the radio had repeated out a warning to other aircraft in the area about our missile engagement. There were still two other Chinooks and an Apache in the area. We landed on one of the parking spots, after putting our load of ammo back from where we had picked it up from some hours earlier, and began shutting down the aircraft. Our engineers were waiting for us eager to check over the aircraft for signs of damage.

The blades stopped and our helmets were off, it was time for the engineers to check everything out. The missile had been close and you never can be too careful so the aircraft would be grounded for a few hours until they were happy with it. As a crew we were all smiling and full of bravado. It was time to get to operations and speak with the Apache pilot. I was wondering what he had seen.

The debriefing session would be massive; only yesterday our intelligence had told us about the Taliban's weapon capabilities, had I missed the SAM brief? We were going to become hot property. When we sat in the back of a Land Rover the co-pilot spoke, "That was the closest I have been to death."

I smiled and laughed, it was the second closest time for me. Operations would be manic so we decided to hold the intelligence debrief in the back our IRT tent. This had to be right, we all needed some quiet, it wasn't about us now, it was about everyone else.

The Taliban had a missile systems and they were trained to use it. It was late when we finally finished debriefing and our aircraft was still impounded while the engineers checked it. The other Chinooks had already left so it was time to thumb a lift on a Hercules back to Kandahar. By the time we handed our kit in and got ourselves back to our rooms, it was nearly 10pm. We had missed dinner but none of us felt like eating.

I entered the accommodation and people were shaking my hand. I was now accepted as part of the team, no longer was I on the outside. Today I had proved myself, the guys were laughing about my baptism of fire. They now had a confidence in me and what I brought to the team. Our boss was nowhere to be seen as he was having high level talks about the events of the day. It was eventually around 11pm when he came into our room and sat at the end of the senior crewman's bed. They discussed the day's events together, I sat up and listened in, I was being talked about as if I was invisible.

The boss wanted to know if we were good to go tomorrow. The senior crewman answered for us both and said we were OK. A 7am briefing was set as there is no sense in delaying it. The boss left us. I laid there awake, was I a part of the team? Not once did he ask if I was OK or if I was good to go.

Over the next two months, so many different things happened that the events of the missile day were cleared out of my head. You have to forget them and move on to the next mission. I had time at Camp Bastian on the IRT, I preferred it there as there were much less politics than Kandahar. We had heard rumours about 'specialist teams' trying to capture the Taliban soldier who had shot the missile at us, but he kept evading them. In the end they will catch up with him, he had spooked a lot of people.

You didn't get shot at during every mission but when you did, it was just another normal day in Afghanistan. It didn't matter what weapon system they shot at you with; AK-47s, RPGs or mortars, you get on with the job. We were there to support the guys on the ground, some days were harder than others, the hardest were dealing with live and dead causalities, especially as the troops were quite young, some not much older than 18 years.

It was just their first years in the army and they were out here performing above and beyond the call of duty. On one IRT mission, the call came in and all of us had to go to operations. This wasn't normal procedure because we usually split so we can get the aircraft running and be in the air quicker. Today the Colonel wanted us all to attend operations, he laid it on the line, a base was taking heavy fire and two of his guys were seriously wounded and needed immediate evacuation. He couldn't guarantee our safety not even with an Apache escort; he asked us all individually if we would go, all of us said yes.

Sadly we just got in the air when the call came in aborting the mission, the two guys had died. Later that night we went in and recovered their bodies; the Colonel had planned to unleash hell on the Taliban who were well dug in, we were clear of the base. I looked behind through the night vision goggles on my helmet. I could see what he meant by hell.

At the end of March we handed over the reins to the next squadron. Our time was over for now, we were going home. When we got back to RAF Odiham, we just dumped our kit in lockers and went on three weeks leave before we had to get ready to go again.

Every tour of duty is different; people remember different aspects from their time away. Loads of other horrific things happened in my time there. I have mentioned just the one that freaked me the most.

It is amazing to look back and perceive at what I thought was everyday normality. It is far from normal everyday life, people who have been there know what I mean. Those of you who haven't, I hope you never have to. This can apply to many different aspects of peoples' lives. It doesn't have to happen in a war zone; trauma is trauma and mine was about to hit me for six, big time.

# CHAPTER TWENTY-FIVE

# PING PONG

I turned the key to my flat and walked in; something didn't feel right. My front room reminded me of when I was married; why had that thought popped into my head?

I looked around, everything appeared normal, it must be jet lag. Nothing a shower and a beer cannot solve, it was time to wash off the last few months and feel normal again.

I cannot put my finger on it; I am just not feeling myself some sort of fog seems to be clouding my brain. Mates joined me for beers, soon sharing war stories of the last few months. Inside I wanted to feel emotion but I couldn't; I am empty. I just need to recharge. I had done operations before, this was different. I knew the answer, keep talking and don't bottle things up. It wasn't the same darkness as before. My brain was starting to flood with thoughts, memories of the last few months and I was empty. There were no emotions attached to any of them.

I had to do something. I needed to feel happy again. Spend money, I thought. I wanted to feel like my home was truly mine. It was time to get rid of the old sofa, pictures and the remaining bits from my marriage. I needed a place I could relax, maybe then some emotions will return. I need a road trip, I'll go and see mates up and down the country.

One thing when you are single, you can do whatever you choose.

Every visit turned out the same, everyone was happy I was home, beers flowed and stories were told. But it was emotionless. I am coping well and feeling good, the hangovers gave me reassurance I was recovering. If I didn't have a beer, memories came back and I lay wide awake with the same question where have my emotions gone?

I had been out a few nights running with my best mate. I had told him everything as usual, there was nothing to shock him.

He turned to me and said that I was talking about the missile too much.

I could see that even he was beginning to get worried So I thought I'll stop talking about it and when I get home I'll go and see my homeopath. She'll sort me, she will understand what's happening.

I had to find some emotions so I planned to start dating again. If I find a chick then I will find my emotions surely? Internet dating sounded perfect. It's a numbers game as you can get knocked backed and hit the delete button, I didn't care, I was empty. The nights were long; I was jumping awake, a loud bang was going off in my head, was I having nightmares?

My leave had come to an end and I was tired even before going back to work. Three weeks of booze and sleepless nights had taken its toll. I had that sinking feeling knowing it was time to work again, but why? I loved flying. Why was I feeling like I don't want to go back? At least my emotions seem to be returning.

I found out my fellow colleagues from Afghanistan were getting debriefed by the medics about Post Traumatic Stress Disorder (PTSD). Two days of different lectures in coping with coming back. I smiled as I thought of them. Most of them would be clock watching wanting them to be over so they could get back to some normal work and get back into the air.

I would swop their briefs for mine, I was attending Guard Commander training, it is dull, I had just spent two months handling weapons. I think I am pretty current in stripping cleaning, loading and unloading but it wasn't for me. As the commander it is your guard force, some may be young and new to the military, I have to keep a close eye on them all, if anything happens it is on my head.

The two days of Guard Commander training are finally over, I am glad to get back to the squadron. I am still tired and the missile is still buzzing in my head, my nights are getting longer with the loud bang disturbing my sleep. I need to chat to my next in command as I had missed the two days of PTSD briefings and thought it best I get them. When I finally track him down, the answer didn't surprise me, "Don't worry mate, you'll be fine, they were a waste of time, go to the pub have a beer!"

I still cannot settle, every day at work is getting harder. I am beginning to hate being in the air. Before Afghanistan I could keep a clear head. Now things keep getting foggy, Afghanistan keeps seeping in, making me lose concentration, what is going wrong with me?

I needed to chat with someone desperately so I phoned my homeopath to make an appointment for the following week. When I get there, I tell her everything about my time away and my lack of emotions. She knows me well and soon is trying a remedy to try and stabilise me. My personal life was going well; it is work where my problems seem to lay. I had started dating and with it found I could detach from my life and be involved with someone else's. With my homeopathic remedy and the gym I am feeling a little normal again, or am I?

The nights are still long. The dating got serious a little too quickly and my new girlfriend and I decided on a holiday. I am throwing my all into it, I don't know why? Maybe it is because Afghanistan is back on the horizon. I knew when my holiday was finished; the training would start again for another detachment out there.

Back at the squadron was the same and my holiday is a distant blur. I have to go away for a few weeks to fly on a course. It is designed to teach aircrew how to become tactical instructors. This is going to mean a lot of missile evasion. On the flight to the training ground with the missile warning systems switched on, the alarm sounds, my heart jumps. I looked out of the window the Apache is alongside, the grey spiralling smoke, and Helmand is below me, I can smell it, the arid air, the heat of the day, the smell of hydraulic fuel and then, the loud bang, my body shudders as the pressure wave passes through me. I look again in disbelief, my eyes must be playing tricks on me, now the UK is below me, what has just happened?

I have to check in and call my quadrant clear; I didn't look and just call it clear, after all this is a UK training mission. As I sit staring out of the window, with every blink I keep expecting things to change, where was I?

My head is spinning from what has just happened am I going mad? Finally we arrived at the base we will be operating from for the next few weeks, As I watch the rotors stopping I am still searching for an answer to what I have just experienced. Maybe I just needed a beer. I can't tell anyone about what has just happened, they will think I am making it up or I am crazy. We are soon heading off to our digs at a base a few miles away, Being busy helped, now all I need to do is get myself sorted for tomorrow and concentrate on what is important, tomorrow's training mission.

The next morning I am feeling tired as the night was

full of Afghanistan and memories of the loud bang. I have to fly, so I can prove to myself that yesterday was an isolated incident. I hide from nothing, if it is hard, do it again until it becomes easy, there is nothing to fear, I am in control. I have to keep my head in the game, for the safety of the crew and the aircraft, that's all what matters.

We were soon in the air and on the ranges and the missile warning alarm sounds, it triggers something in me yet again and I go back to February 13th the day of the missile. I start sweating, shaking, I cannot let anyone see this, this isn't me. We get back I need the gym, I have to feel about something other than Afghanistan. It isn't fear, it is something I cannot figure out, I want to push my body to it's limits and to feel normal again. Fear eventually arrives when I go to bed, I don't want to close my eyes, if I am awake I can control what is going on. I have to make some tough choices. I am becoming dangerous in the air, if I cannot control my head I could hurt someone, something may go wrong.

My alarm sounds 7am, today is a rerun of yesterday's training mission. I have to go, I can do this, I need to keep control today. I will not put anyone's safety in jeopardy because of me and my stupid head, they are only memories, vivid ones, but memories nonetheless. I am keeping control well, nothing has happened, no Apache and no Helmand. I knew it was an isolated incident, and then a grey spiral. I look again, it is there, I am not imagining it, the UK and grey smoke spiralling.

The team controlling the ranges have a special firework which enables aircrew to see what a spiralling missile looks like. I had missed the radio call warning me it was coming, maybe because I am so focused on keeping everyone safe and not going back to Afghanistan. This is the last thing I need.

I look again and it is there again, the Apache, Helmand, I tense my body waiting for the pressure wave to pass through me. Sweat is pouring out of me, I shake and then I hear the crew talking on the intercom, they are asking my opinion on the firework and if it is a true representation of a real missile.

We land and I set off for my safe place the gym, even here I cannot stop thinking about today. One more set and it will go away, it doesn't, another set and another the pain passes through me as my muscles scream for me to stop exercising. It finally has gone and is replaced with pain, satisfied I head back to the accommodation. I need to answer some questions, I need a beer and I need to do some soul searching, can I keep doing this to myself?

I look at my watch 3.45am, I have a few hours before I have to get up. I phoned my girlfriend earlier to tell her I had made a decision, I had got emotional about it, it is a life changing decision and I wanted her to be the first to know. It is time to leave the military and run, today I am going to hand in my notice to leave. It's called PVR - Premature Voluntary Release - and it will take 18 months. I will work out my time and do the detachments. A few will be in Afghanistan but it doesn't matter, nothing does, I am not safe if I can't control my mind.

When we arrive at the base, I hunt down the detachment commander, an old friend from when we were both flying on the same squadron. I unload and fall apart in tears. It is pointless holding back, I tell him everything that I have been living with and experiencing when I am in the air and that I had made a decision to leave. It was time to run.

He looks at me, his eyes understand, his voice is calming He tells me it's OK for me to leave the detachment and return to Odiham. It takes a few hours to drive back, all the time I keep thinking about my last 14 years of military life.

Sod my pension I am signed up on a 22 year contract but I feel I am unsafe. My head keeps wandering but it returns to the same thing, I will not risk the safety of others, I have to quit.

I pull into the squadron, my palms are sweaty, I have to find my boss and explain what is going on. I finally track him down and we go to his office. For the second time I explain what has been going on in my head for the last few months. He is new in post, taking command just a few weeks ago, I bet this is the last thing he was expecting.

I finish and he starts, I have to go to the doctors as he thinks I may be unwell and he refuses to accept my decision to quit until I have been seen by the doctor. He doesn't finish there, he thinks it is my past coming back to haunt me. He was new here, why had someone dragged my past into it? It is behind me; why hadn't the squadron moved on too? I only met this guy a few weeks ago, he said we all can have a clean sheet. Well, where is mine?

I get home and my place feels empty despite the makeover I gave it when I returned from Afghanistan. I decide not to tell my girlfriend I am back, I need to be alone tonight. I have to get control of myself and make my boss see sense. It is not my past. If he had been involved in my darkness he would have known it. I simply have to get him to accept my decision to leave on a PVR.

I lay awake not wanting to close my eyes and a little fear crept in. I had had enough of thinking about Afghanistan today, I didn't want to dream about it too, not tonight. My eyes feel heavy and I close them, but they are soon woken by a loud bang going off inside me.

The doctor has changed at Odiham but I still have a good relationship with her. She knows about my past because she arrived as it all came to a close. My previous doctor had also convinced me she needed to know as he had been posted away to a new RAF station. I am glad she does because she knows the real me. Instantly she knew I wasn't myself, I sit and speak about the last few months and what I had been experiencing and now I wanted to leave and run from it. She listens and then asks me to do something, not just for me but to help others like me; she knew people were leaving the force early because they were experiencing similar problems.

She wants the military system to be accountable for what has happened to me and others in Afghanistan and to make sure we are going to get the right help. But, and there is always a but, I have to be brave enough to hold my hands up and tell the system that I am having real problems. She has to refer me to Department of Community Mental Health (DCMH) for assessment. Then we have to tell them about my overdose and the private work I have done to overcome my past. I am conflicted about going back to DCMH as the last time I was there, their answer to everything was anti-depressant tablets and six months off flying.

So I talk everything through with the doctor, the pros and cons, she knows I am happy to leave the service and to go back to Afghanistan as I work out my PVR notice. But she is my doctor and I trust her judgement she always has had my best interest and welfare at heart. In the past, she has never given me a reason not to trust her. With that I agree to stand up and be counted by the system not just for me, but for others like me who are suffering and won't come forward. She places me on two weeks sick leave so I can try to stabilise my sleep patterns and relax without the constant reminders from the Chinooks.

I head for home, feeling numb, she had mentioned Post Traumatic Stress Disorder (PTSD) but she cannot give me a diagnosis because she isn't a psychiatrist. I have to wait for an appointment with the specialists of DCMH.

The next two weeks I tried to make myself forget, but things keep triggering me. I live near the base and the Chinook's distinctive sound is enough to send my head into images of Afghanistan. The more I tried to get control, the more I couldn't, it was one stupid mission, why was it that one? What about the other things I'd seen - the injured, the dead, the near-dead - why didn't I remember them? Why was it just that missile?

Two weeks had passed and I went back to see the doctor and thankfully she saw that I needed to work. Being at home alone isn't good for me, I just get trapped in my head. She is happy for me to return to work and fly again. We still hadn't had a response from DCMH but she will chase them up for me. It feels odd walking into the squadron, people are getting ready for the return to Afghan. I need to get ready too I still want to go with the team; I don't want to let anyone or myself down.

First I need to chat with my boss, I tell him I hadn't seen the specialists yet, but I am happy and I have been cleared to fly. He looks straight through me, I was about to realise why I'd felt weird about coming back in, "I don't want you here around the squadron, until I know you are not lying about this. Until you have been seen by the specialist and we know where we stand. Go back to the doctors and get signed off work."

Did I just hear him right? Lying? It then returned, a spark inside, I had felt anger like this before; he had ignited me. Keep control, I have to, for his sake. I take myself away in shock at what I just had heard, I had to wait a while as doctors are always busy and I already had had one appointment today. I am sure she could feel my anger or she could see it in my face as I walked in her office, closing the door behind me. She phones my boss and leaves him in no illusion I was fit for duty. I am starting to feel like a ping pong ball, getting batted from one side to the other.

So I headed back to the squadron to be greeting with, "Go home on gardening leave until after your appointment with the specialists."

The feelings inside were getting stronger, was I a liar, or was I infectious? What is wrong with these people? I thought we were a team. I knew what I had to do, the only way to deal with this spark was to extinguish it, with pain, I needed to feel pain, the gym will level me out.

Days go past, I keep the feelings away from my girlfriend and she is spending most nights at my place. When we go to bed, I don't sleep, fear of Afghanistan is polluting my dreams and the anger of being called a liar by my squadron, keep me awake. During the days I channel all the feelings into the gym, my head is going off in different directions, it is hard to stay still. The new emotion of guilt starts to race through my veins, I was letting the team down.

My specialist appointment finally arrives. I am nervous, I have started to doubt myself, I have started to believe my boss, was I lying? I filled in the tests and chatted with the 'expert' for an hour. He has my notes and my doctor's referral, so it is pointless covering anything up. I give him full disclosure about Afghanistan and my past. He soon realises my past has been dealt with, he is only interested in my last six months since returning from operations in Afghanistan.

His diagnosis of what is happening with my head, Post Traumatic Stress Response (PTSR) and I needed to be treated quickly otherwise I could develop the full blown Disorder. Who knows what the difference is?

A feeling of relief warms my insides, now I know I wasn't lying. He is still talking, best I concentrate on what he is saying, I tune back into the conversation. Due to having PTSR and because I am aircrew, I am unfit to fly or to carry any weapons for six months. My heart sinks and the warm feeling is turned to instant ice cold. What had he just done?

Yet again my job had been taken away, hadn't he listened, everyone will again think I am war dodging.

Thoughts race through my head as I drive away, I am driving, but not really aware of anything around me. I am numb, I wasn't lying but I am yet again unable to do my job. I have to find my boss and tell him the news. This should at least shut him up, but what do I do now?

I have to explain to people but they don't want to listen, already I am on the outside looking in. My emotions are all over the place. I had PTSR, now what?

Make me better, I need to stop thinking, my head is spinning, having a label isn't helping. It has given people something to talk about, I shut myself away from the staring eyes and whispering voices into an office. I need this sorting, I need my head straight.

# CHAPTER TWENTY SIX

# COWARD

I started to tumble over the next few weeks as I have lost the support from my doctor, who has been sent away on operations. My friendly face and most of my other allies at Odiham will be away for six months. I have to fight alone.

I still haven't heard back from DCMH about starting some form of treatment, sleep is more miss than hit, I am beginning to get edgy around people, I have to keep one thing stable in my life, I need to cling onto my relationship, I need something good in my life. I need to beat this and return to work, my focus has changed, I don't want to leave the military. I will prove myself once more to the squadron; I can bounce back from absolutely anything. My nightmares are getting worse and my dread of the base is increasing everyday. The days I do make it in I keep myself shut away. If I go to the crew room, people won't engage with me in the same way. The first few of my colleagues have started to return to Afghanistan, it is unbearable to watch. Everyone seems to be moving around and I am in slow motion. Was I being brave for admitting to this problem or should I have kept quiet?

The base has finally broken me. Some days I sit outside in my car unable to take myself through the gates. Both the people and the Chinooks I have to avoid at all costs and maybe this will help in controlling my brain and stop any memories about February 13th. The memories are starting to darken. This isn't happening again, I will not go back to a dark place.

Weeks have passed since I was diagnosed and still no help or word from DCMH. This was just what I expected from the military system. I need help, they are letting me down again, I will have to sort it myself.

I have stopped going into work. I had to so I could stop the images and feelings of Afghanistan, best I call my boss. As I dial the number, I wonder if they have noticed I haven't been there. When I put the receiver down, I'd had it confirmed - no one had noticed my absence. I have asked to be moved out of Odiham, not forever just until I get my head sorted, as there are other ground jobs I can do at other bases. I offered to help to write the aircrew manual, anything to keep me busy. I need to distract my head, stop any form of dark thoughts, stop this hijacking by Afghanistan.

I distract myself with cleaning my flat, I can clean it for hours, everything has to be in place, if I know where everything is I cannot get upset. If my girlfriend moves something I have to put it back. I can't abide mess. Am I becoming obsessive compulsive? My bed is slowly becoming a place of fear, I hate closing my eyes, if my head has a chance to remind me about events it does.

Finally my treatment is starting, I sit in the waiting room. It is a cold room with a TV, a fish tank and leaflets, mainly about drinking and relationships. A guy walks in, in uniform, glasses, the balding, physique of a once rugby player who has rounded over the years. He introduces himself to me; he is to become my new CPN. I am expected to immediately trust this guy and share everything with him. I want answers and quick, I need to be back in the air. I need a job to focus on things away from my feelings.

He explains a process he wants to use on me, a thing called Eye Movement Desensitisation and Reprocessing (EMDR). I am sceptical but I have to let him try, anything is better than what is happening.

The appointment lasts an hour and, in the end, we didn't try the EMDR. I just cannot understand why I should just be expected to let him in, just because he wears the same uniform and works at DCMH. I know we are all experts in our own field, but I am not getting a good feeling about this guy. I have to give him a chance and I will, I owe myself that.

On the second day at DCMH, I walk in to the waiting room and sat behind the door is a pilot I know. My heart sinks, I don't want to engage with him but we spent 12 months flying together. He looks as uncomfortable as me. Both of us agree in not letting people know we have seen each other here as he is getting signed fit today. I don't know his story but he thinks he should be back in the air very soon. I have to be seen by the physiatrist who diagnosed me with PTSR. My treatment will be overseen by him because of my job as aircrew.

His opening line made me smile "How was my treatment going?"

I am not intimidated by him so I answer, "What treatment? I was only seen yesterday."

He shifts uncomfortably in his chair and begins to fluster, "That shouldn't have happened."

I know that for six weeks I had got worse since he gave me a label and took my job away. I discuss an assignment change away from the Chinooks, I explain how hard it is for me to cross the threshold of the camp gates without my thoughts and feelings being hijacked.

"It is counter productive to do that," he says.

"Is this guy listening to what has happened to me over the last six weeks?" I wonder.

I just want a purpose and reason to fight, surely it is in the best interest of the service to keep a sergeant employed and not have him go mad alone at home? The appointment finishes and I am shown the door, these people haven't changed since I was last seen by them years ago, they pretend to listen, he didn't seem to hear a word I said.

I get home to my phone ringing, a boss from Odiham, maybe they will help me? The usual pleasantries. Come on get on with it, I am not in the mood today DCMH have just rattled my cage, I need some good news.

"We cannot move you. The best thing the squadron can do for you is leave you at home. Come in if you feel strong enough, but you are on gardening leave."

Did I just hear him correct? I am to stay here, why are all these people doing this to me? Just give me a purpose, a job, make me feel a part of something, stop punishing me for admitting to thinking about Afghanistan. You sent me there, now help me, please. I have been deserted by almost everyone, I have to keep what was happening away from my relationship. My increasing agitation is not her fault; I think she won't leave me if I protect her from it and from me.

Bonfire night is imminent, already I am feeling fear of what may happen to me. The loud bangs, the colours of the fireworks, reminding me of tracer bullets. It will be a tiring week, why do people start celebrations early and finish them late when bonfire night is only meant to last one day?

Everywhere I go, I am getting more agitated, crowds, shopping, this week has unnerved me, the only peace I am getting is from the pain of exercise. Even going to Tesco I have to mentally prepare myself. I don't want to see or be seen by anyone. I can see the door, someone is walking towards me, I recognise that face, a colleague we flew together in the past, best I be social, but a brave face on it.

So I wave at him, he turns and looks me straight in the eye and says, "Coward."

I am stunned, it was exactly what I didn't need to hear, what do I do, shall I fill him in?

No, keep control use it, use it like you have done before. I turn, Tesco can wait. I need to go to the gym and quick, I need some pain to balance me out again.

I was right. Bonfire night was hell, a constant reminder. Like I needed any more reminders but they keep coming. A few days later, I saw a fellow crewman in the street; he started to rip into me asking if I was still cowering behind the sofa because of fireworks. I may have been able to take the banter or black humour, but my head is full, I am tired. Is this what people really think of me?

# CHAPTER TWENTY SEVEN

# DO IT YOURSELF

The appointments with DCMH are nauseatingly boring. They involve me sitting and chatting about my week. I find that's easy. The noise of Chinooks and loud bangs make my mind flood with Afghanistan. In the more intense moments, I can see it, feel it and smell it. It is always there, never going away.

We have started the EMDR treatment and it is horrible. I am made to remember Afghanistan in its entirety. I want to escape from it not relive it. My body has started to show signs of stress with nose bleeds. After only a few sessions, they decided it wasn't for me. Now I have a new task, I have to write down every detail of the mission in Afghanistan and put it on my coffee table.

Every time I walk by it, I have to pick it up and read it. Why wasn't he listening to me? Why are you making me relive this thing? I am on a merry go round and I cannot stop it. Every six weeks I check in with the physiatrist and he thinks my treatment is going well. I am sure he has the wrong notes in front of him. I am getting worse, it is happening more, not less and it is intensifying. I have to continually balance myself with the gym so I don't let things spill into my relationship.

I am beginning to get suspicious again as what is being

reported back, it seems to be very different to what we talk about in my treatment sessions. My coffee table has become another place in my flat to avoid. Before just my bedroom was where my head got hijacked. The diary of the mission is on my table. I want to scream but who would hear? Who would care?

Christmas is here, it arrived packed full of emotions. It has been months since I have spoken with work, my treatment isn't going well. I am keeping a lid on me by using the gym hard. My relationship is going OK, I think. Maybe I have been kidding myself, between the gym and some days a hangover, I have been hurting her. She was the one person I thought I was protecting. I walk into the bedroom and she is lying on the bed, tears flowing from her eyes. My heart sinks, what is wrong?

She looks at me and it all comes out. She has seen my pain and cannot help me, she feels useless. By protecting her I am just hurting her because I am hiding any emotions from her. All she sees is me constantly hitting the gym, tidying and fussing about the flat or drinking.

It is the kick up the arse I needed. I hate myself for hurting her, it is time to take control of this and sort out some proper treatment away from DCMH. I phoned my homeopath immediately. I had spoken with DCMH about homeopathy I was told to keep it quiet as they didn't believe in it.

Why won't they just support my steps in getting me better? It has worked before why not now?. I am getting worse. My CPN is finally opening his eyes and seeing it. He hands me a book about trying to understand PTSD, he says it may help me and my girlfriend to understand a little more.

It is an easy read, I haven't read in months as my concentration has left me. Written in black and white, on the pages of the book, are every emotion and feeling I have. Essentially, I am staring back at myself from the pages of a book. The person who wrote this understands a little about PTSD, but it is all centred around the civilian world, not my military one.

In it there was an example of a desensitisation programme, a car accident is given as an example. Some victims of car accidents cannot face getting into a car again. They have to start by looking at the car, then opening the door, then sitting in it, before finally driving again. The process takes as long as it takes, but you keep building yourself up. I decided I have to try, I make a plan. If DCMH were not helping, I will help myself and I will beat this once and for all.

I start by driving to Odiham again. Some days it can take several trips and hours to get through the gates. I cannot bump into anyone; I feel everyone thinks I am a coward. When I get there, I sit in my car, in the car park next to the airfield and watch the helicopters, experiencing the sights and sounds. If I manage to park close enough the downwash of a Chinook passing, shudders my car and the distinctive sound sends me straight back.

Most days end the same, I end up vomiting or in tears as the feelings and images get stronger, the more emotional I get the more it drives me to sit it out. No pain no gain. I decide I better tell my CPN about it. He thinks it is a great idea and to keep at it; why didn't he come up with it or help me do it?

The next stage in my DIY treatment plan is to go back to my squadron and see my old colleagues now they are all back from Afghanistan. It takes a few times, I drive through the car park, not wanting to stop outside the front door. I park up, sweaty, heart beating, I have to keep control. I go through a little breathing ritual I use when I am going for a heavy set in the gym; this focuses me on the task in hand.

I open the door and stride out of the car, my eyes are fixed on the squadron, the door leading to the stairs. I want to go straight to the big boss's office first, I owed him that much as I still respected his rank. I wanted him to know I was back on his squadron.

On the way to his door, an old friend appears, we start to chat; he tells me I should keep going with it, as it will be worth a few quid in the end! He thinks this is a game, a ploy to get money from the system, how can he think this? I don't want anything except my head back, I want my job back, I want to be normal again, stuff your money!

My emotions start to spin, if I am not careful I will have to turn back to the car and run, no I won't let this thought stop me. I know there will always be one smart arse with an opinion that I was in it for the cash or I was making a meal of it. They simply don't know or care. I finally get to my boss's office, he looks shocked and surprised I am there. Just tapping on his door is challenge enough for one day though. We chat for just a while before a Chinook starts and he sees me disappear into myself. Inside I am already hearing the bang and feeling the pressure wave. I am completely exhausted and need to go home and recharge.

The year is marching on, I am still pushing hard to fix myself, not just for me but for my girlfriend too. She sees how much effort I am putting into this. Some days when she comes around, I don't want to move off the sofa. I cannot even muster the energy to go to the gym because the music and flashing strobe lights would send my mind back off to Afghanistan.

I need to focus on my own DIY desensitisation. I decide it is time for my next step, even though just getting to the squadron was hard, I have to make things harder, it was time to start flying again. I pass the idea through my CPN, he is delighted with my decision. I will ask the squadron if

I can book a simulator flight. He wants two, one hour slots separated by an hour, the first hour will be a flight around Hampshire the area I am familiar with, the second hour will be the Afghan database.

I froze, he wants to do what? Back to Afghanistan, I thought we did things slowly; my mind was starting to melt with the thoughts of going back. I have to do this though. I have to do what he wants because finally he is taking interest in what I am doing. I will have to organise it, but it will be another hurdle in getting better. I phone the squadron and request the two simulator hours. I asked for specific crew who are friends knowing they won't judge me if things go wrong.

I have to lay down, I have tried to go out for the day, I need to distract myself because tomorrow I am in the simulator. My head is in a constant battle with images of Afghanistan and fear about tomorrow. I start to feel faint again, I have had already had to sit down several times today because I was about to collapse. I am lucky I know my body so well from pushing hard in the gym. I know the signs. My skin goes clammy, my breathing shallows and then I start looking through a tunnel. If the sides are black, the tunnel closes and I collapse.

I am still dizzy, the night has been long and restless, I have to go to the simulator, what is troubling me? Is it the simulator or is it my uniform?

I haven't worn one in nine months and now I am off flying, going to a busy crew room and wearing the uniform. My heart starts to pound, it feels as if it will beat a hole in my chest, sweat is pouring off me. I cannot go, I need to cancel, I cannot drive there like this. I phone my CPN and explain what is going on; his advice makes me angry; it is only an anxiety attack, he tells me just to drive slowly and carefully.

This guy is starting to really piss me off, why won't he listen? The tunnel, the blackness, I have to control it or I will faint. I call a friend, one of the crew who is flying the simulator for me, he aggress it is a dumb idea to drive so he will collect me as it will be safer for everyone. When we arrive at the building, I need to compose myself. I haven't managed to wear my uniform yet, it is a symbol to me and I don't know if I can put it on feeling this way. I am a disgrace and I shouldn't wear it.

When I enter the building, there are aircrew mates flitting about, I look out of place without a uniform. I head to the bathroom so I can change, I need to blend in. My hands shake as I pull up the zip on my flying suit. I walk into the crew room and my CPN is there. I feel everyone's eyes are watching me but I scan the room and there is no one I recognise. Good, now compose myself. Don't show this lot what I have become, a quick brew and it is time.

We all walk down to the simulator together, I hang back trying to control my breathing and my head. I need to regain some sanity and this should help. The ramp of the simulator we are using is down, we can go straight in. Focus, I can do this, it is only a simulator. As I enter the visual screens show the parking dispersal from Odiham; I am taking the crewman's seat in the back. On my screen the Chinook is pictured on it, we are all strapped in and then guys at the front start the proceedings. As soon the noise and vibration come on, I have to get out, my head is going to explode, images fly through me, my body is under constant attack from a pressure wave from the past. I am trapped, the ramp is up, I start to sweat, my breathing is getting heavier as panic starts to bite into me. I have to get out at all costs.

I know if I open the door that the system will shut down completely. It doesn't matter I need out. My CPN stands up, this guy may think he is big but I am in no mood. My look says it all so he thinks differently and sits back down. The simulator instructor is getting the ramp down as quick as he can, as soon as I hear the clank of it engaging, I open the door and run. I am going to puke.

I go for the nearest bathroom and heave as soon as I am in distance of the toilet bowl. I sit there, shaking, on the toilet floor. I hear the door go to the bathroom, a tap on the door of the cubical I am sat in; it is my CPN. He starts to spout some bollocks; if he wants to see me rage, he is pushing the right buttons. I fly out of the cubical. I can feel it flowing through me, pure rage. What did it for me was the shit he was saying about letting myself down by having to leave the simulator.

A voice of reason screams from my insides, don't do it, you are better than this control it. My look says it all for the second time, he leaves me to it. I have to get control, I reach into my pocket I had brought my iPod, I plug in and spend what seems like hours trying to calm myself. I decide I can clear this hurdle and beat it, with my music playing I go back to the simulator. I say nothing as I walk past my CPN now stood outside, I march straight in, strap in leaving my music playing and signalled I am ready to try this again.

For the next 30 minutes I undergo a constant wave of flashbacks. I have a stuck DVD in my head, playing the same scene repeatedly. The screens go black, the noise stops, that was the first hour over, it feels longer, I feel completely drained. I am not going back in today and definitely not going for the Afghan database. Today I am beat.

My regular doctor and friendly face has returned from her tour away, I am glad she is back and immediately arrange an appointment. Even going to Odiham to see her poses as a challenge. It has been a week since the simulator and I have gone backwards. The nightmares and flashbacks have increased.

I am finding it hard to keep control of anything, the only solitude I find is spending hours alone cycling. I know I simply have to see her even if it takes several attempts to get through the camp gates. When I finally manage to get in front of her, I tell her what has been going on for the last six months while she has been away. She is disgusted I had just been left at home and says she'll sort this out.

The squadron organises an internal transfer for me. I don't care what they do to me anymore, they all think the same thing. They'd justified it to my doctor, telling her it will give me a stable base and that my team are too busy to have someone like me on their books.

Thankfully my new boss is one of the good guys, a friend from old we shared some great times together before he was promoted and posted. Now he's back to command his own section, he is a real people person and he genuinely wants me back to full fitness. If anyone can help me with the problems I have within the squadron he can and will. I still want to return to my career, I want my sanity back, I want to get on with life this has been going on too long.

Between us we book several simulator flights, this time will be different we will take it very slowly. My new boss will fly them all for me and we'll go at my speed. I am glad I have him in my corner, with him and my doctor back in control of my welfare at Odiham, I can see things changing for me. I am not battling alone.

When we start the simulator trips together, he always collects me. The drive takes about an hour, it is the perfect time to chat about everything. It soon becomes clear to him that we need to get me back involved in squadron life and show people what has happened. It will also show me not everyone has opinions of me and those who do show them it is they who are wrong.

We start slow, despite my CPN insisting on going at it

like a bull in a china shop, my boss won't let him because this is about me getting fit again, not him. Some days, when I am having a bad one with flashbacks, we leave the ramp down and door open so I can get out if needed. Some days we don't have sound, my boss is more understanding than my CPN. I am now in the co-pilots seat. My boss is even sharpening his own instructor experience by teaching me how to fly. I am distracted in learning to fly yet he notices around 3000 feet I am constantly checking over to my left, I am subconsciously looking for a missile.

The simulator flights are finally getting easier, after each one I am not left zombie-like on the sofa. We decide it is time for the second part of our plan. I need to push my limits again, things are too comfortable. I am going to return to work at the squadron. My boss agrees to mornings only and I will help his section in training new Chinook aircrew. There is admin I can get on with and he is there to give me the top cover if anyone decides to give me a hard time.

It is good to get some sort of normality back, some days after real hard nights, I cannot make it to work but I call in and chat about it, those days are getting fewer. In the interest of even more normality, I propose to my girlfriend; she accepts and moves in. The glimmer of an ending to this thing seems to be in sight and now I have a fiancée to consider it drives me harder.

I have to constantly push things, even though at times I push myself too hard and I would be sick or have a few days without sleep. It is a small price to pay to try to regain my sanity. My boss is heading off on a training mission. I am feeling good, I am going to do it, another step, a real Chinook. I will sit on board while they start and get off before they leave. I start to get sweaty as I talk it over with my boss, he asks if I am sure. I say I am, I can do this, this will make me better.

I strap in on the sidewall seats, the distinct hydraulic and fuel smell of the Chinook, I am sat on the left, next to the same window I looked out of and saw the missile. My mind drifts off, a pressure wave passes through me. I look up, the crewman is giving me the thumbs up, we are about to start. I grip the seat, I have to sit this out, I reach for a sick bag, I am going to chuck. I breathe through the feelings, the first engine has started, the rotor break is been released, the Chinook shake starts as it spins up to speed. I want to run, my mind and body are under constant attack from Afghanistan.

The second engine sparks into life, just a few more minutes, I have the sick bag squeezed so tight my knuckles are white. My flying suit is dripping in sweat, the start up procedures are completed, I get the thumbs up to leave. As I stand my legs are shaking, I grab the rail and shuffle down to the ramp area, a deep breath and I get off the Chinook. A few meters past and the downwash and exhaust fumes hit me, my legs are weak. I just have the strength to push back and stop myself falling. Thankfully no one is around. I let the tears flow out, that maybe was a step too far.

I get to my car still shaking from the start up. I will take my helmet home today. The tunnel closes around me. I come around with the steering wheel in front of me. I have to get home. I need to be far away from here. I turn the key and shaking I put it into reverse and start my journey to the relative safety of my flat.

I make it home and drop onto the sofa; this is me for the day, the phone rings later it is my boss checking in. Was I OK?

I tell him I am drained and it was tough, I need time to process what happened. My fiancée returns from work to find me curled up in the same position on the sofa. Not understanding what I have been through today she wants to talk, I don't, just leave me to it today. Today I have been lost in a constant wave of flashbacks. It takes me a week to level out again from starting the aircraft, but I will go back for more, I have to. It will make me better.

Finally I get to a healthy working relationship with my CPN. I don't know why it has taken this long but it has. He has just left me to it these last months with my own DIY desensitisation programme. I tell him what I am planning and what I have done. He doesn't advise me either way, so I must be doing things well. He delivers some news, he is leaving at short notice to a new appointment somewhere further north. This is a blow because I have decided to embark into flying for real. First on holiday to Spain and then on the Chinook. I was really hoping he would join me for the Chinook flight.

# Chapter Twenty eight

# The Question

We are due to fly off on holiday tomorrow. I am having the same faint feelings, my head is all over the place. I feel sick with a constant wave of memories about Afghanistan engulfing me.

I am starting to feel angry, what the hell is wrong with me? So I go and get my bike, I have to get out and control this and shake it off. So I set off for a long hard ride, that will control me, I will stop feeling this way. Why has my head mixed flying on holiday with flying on operations?

Every little thing seems to be sending me straight back into thoughts about Afghanistan. Is it the airport, the aircraft or people? I had totally ruined the holiday by the time I had controlled my emotions about getting there. I was a mess for the day after we landed and the day before we were due to return home. I was unpleasant to talk to or to be around. I got snappy because I am lost inside my head, desperately trying to keep control of it. I thought we had an understanding my fiancée and I. I have started to talk about everything but she has started to pick on other things like my need for tidiness. It destroyed our holiday together, she seems to be making an excuse about every emotion I feel. Why she cannot accept it is just Afghanistan I don't know. I don't know how much more she can take.

I am due to go away with the squadron and the more I think about it, the more stressed I am getting. My emotions are still raw from the holiday and now I was going away again. I will be with colleagues 24/7 and I hope they at least will understand what is happening.

I still have the determination to push, I will get back in the air, things will get better. We are going to work at a different air base, no one there knows me, so I can try to get on with it. I will have no CPN support, he has left and I don't have a replacement. It is up to me and my boss.

I'll start slow, first I will attempt aircraft starts. I will try to do one a day, no matter how bad it makes me feel. I keep doing it, I am beginning to feel real tired, I am getting little or no sleep. Afghanistan keeps me awake. Sitting at work, I keep drifting off, but the loud bang and pressure wave soon bring me back. I have to try and take the next step, it is time to fly. I am scheduled for the afternoon. I need to keep busy and distract my brain so I grab my gym kit. I constantly clock watch, waiting for my boss to return. I hear it land, my heart jumps, my eyes glaze over with tears. What the hell?

I find myself standing outside, waiting for them to taxi back in and pick me up. I stand shaking, I have my helmet on, it makes no difference, even this cannot protect me. A thumbs up from the crewman, my signal to approach the aircraft, I take a deep breath. I pull down my dark visor, everyone on this detachment have been told what a big a step this is for me. I enter the aircraft the crewman instructor has the jump seat ready for me, in between the two pilots. I plug into the intercom, my boss says a few words but they are lost on me. We taxi out, I am in constant vigilance, scanning expecting the inevitable to happen. My stomach is on a spin cycle, we are just doing a quick circuit around the base. I have to close my eyes to control my thoughts, I am in the UK not Afghanistan but, as I open my eyes, Afghanistan is again below me. I brace as the pressure wave passes through me, a tear rolls down my cheek. We are on finals to land, it will be over soon. As we walk away from the aircraft I feel ashamed and disgusted with myself, one time I was hanging out the back and now I am a quivering wreck just sat as excess baggage along for the ride.

Again I cannot settle, the flight has unnerved me. It is OK though, I will bounce back. I always do. Every time I close my eyes, a film of Afghanistan plays back. The more I try to control it, the clearer it becomes and with it the feeling of guilt; why couldn't I let it go? Why didn't I think about the truly dangerous stuff? Why not the dead bodies? Why this one event?

I cannot close my eyes, I don't want to drink booze because it makes it worse, training is the only way. I have to hurt, the training endorphin rush keeps me awake for longer. I will fly again this week, I will beat this. I will get fixed no matter what. No longer will people believe I am a coward or that I'm weak. I will be strong again.

For today though, it was time to admit defeat and go home. I am completely drained, day and night my thoughts are hijacked with the same images and feelings. I have sat on several starts and I have flown twice. It is not good enough, I feel broken, I have failed to fix myself, the failure floats into my head and starts to spin and mix with all the other stuff in there.

It is no better at home, my fiancée has had about enough of me. I can sense it, everything seems to annoy either one of us. I have tried it her way and to share what I am feeling, now it is back to the way which works. I need to isolate her from me. I insist everything is spotless and everything has a place, I watch her prepare a salad. She slices a tomato in a different direction to how I do it. How could she? She knows

I need everything perfect. The rage hit me hard and caught me off balance.

I get my trainers go for a run, a hard run; she cannot see me this way. As I lace my trainers, my hands are shaking. I have to protect her from me, she won't understand what had just happened. How can I explain it to her if I didn't know what was happening myself?

She comes into the corridor as I open the door. Our eyes meet and she looks confused at why I am off without saying a word. I force out a smile, wave my hand and close the door, just go, run, run hard, run until I either puke or the pain stops me.

I need help again so I call the doctor and make an appointment. We discuss the last week and she is impressed about how much I did but I still feel a failure. I still don't have a CPN, she will sort it and picks up the phone to DCMH. Within minutes she is talking to my new case worker and an appointment has been made for the following week. I have to admit defeat again with my battle and accept some sleeping pills, just to stabilise me. I needed sleep, it didn't matter if it was chemically induced. I hated tablets but I didn't have a choice; anything that will settle my head and stop the nightmares, just for a day will be good.

My doctor is frank with me, she thinks it is time for me to stop fighting to fly Chinooks and concentrate on me. She will discuss things with my boss and compile a report about me and send it my psychiatrist. They know how hard I have been pushing and now I am broken and need sleeping pills. They want him to know what we have been doing to try to beat this and to maybe just reassign me for a while until I am strong enough for helicopters again.

The sleeping tablets do their job, but when they wear off I'm awake with the same thoughts. I have to meet my new CPN, someone else I have to try and build a relationship with, someone else I have to let in. Within minutes of the door closing, I knew she was going to be different from the one before. She has something about her. She seems to understand trauma at a more personal level. I have no doubts with her; I spill out every thought and emotion of the past 17 months, since the incident in Afghanistan.

She sat and listened, she is motivated and reviewed my treatment and she then decided I needed structure. I was pushing hard without guidance, it was too much. I needed to take a step back and go back to basics. Together we formulated a plan, I needed to know why the missile had got so close and why I now associated being in the air with a missile. If I got some answers maybe then I could move on. A plan was formulated to get me answers and then we would go back to flying, first on the trainers and then back to the Chinook. She promised to be there every step of the way to guide me through.

I was pleased, finally after nearly ten months of treatment with DCMH, something was about to happen. The excitement grew inside, another glimmer of light in this never ending tunnel of nightmares and flashbacks. Maybe my head will become clear and I will again be able to sleep without fear but most of all I will be back in the air doing a job I love.

My excitement soon turned to disappointment at the next meeting with my psychiatrist. I shook his hand and walked into his office; I had got some balance back and was excited about working with my new CPN from the department. Placed on his desk in my line of sight were the two reports one from my doctor and the second from my boss. No matter where I enter I always check out my surroundings, I have to be alert, it helps me to control my brain. I don't get any unwanted surprises this way.

He sits behind his desk in uniform, his tone and manner

have changed from our previous appointments. He seems more aggressive towards me, it felt like someone has been messing with his train set; that would be my doctor and my boss. I need him to give me a chance, I have a plan, a plan from one of his staff, but every time I suggest anything, his answer is no. I am getting frustrated, I need to show him how much a structured programme means to me; he doesn't care. I was about to say something else to counter his no, a compromise which will hopefully keep us both happy, but he isn't in the mood to hear it.

He tells me I have to stop everything, no more getting on board Chinooks, no more pushing my limits. I was simply suffering from depression and I have to take medication. The hate spread through my veins quicker than I could have imagined. I started to flush, I wanted to explode, this guy sat here and was telling me I am depressed. Why was he telling me this? Is he trying to provoke a reaction?

His talk is all about the tablets, the anti-depressants, he is treating me like I am an idiot. His tone and manner are very condescending. Every word he spits out seems to have a vile meaning or undertone. The hate pumps through me even more, I knew they would do this to me in the end. This is all they have to offer, tablets. They don't contain me and don't treat me. If I had structured treatment programme from the start I may not be feeling this way. I knew if he made me take them, it would be a minimum of six months, which would be me finished. I will have then been on the ground for over 18 months.

As I sit across from him, he is talking but I am lost. My career is disappearing before my eyes. All my life is gone in this one conversation. He says it without an ounce of remorse. I switch back in to what he is saying, it rattles me deep, I want to vomit. He isn't bothered about me, his concern is for the RAF. In my eyes he is no longer my doctor, but another uniform who is stopping me getting better. Our doctor patient relationship was over.

I left the appointment, raging with hate inside, this guy, who the hell did he think he was? Depressed, another six months before I had a chance of getting back in the air, no more desensitisation programme, I am lost on the inside. All my hope has gone, will I ever get better?

My only comfort now is spending hours alone on my bike. At all costs I must avoid all situations that reminded me of Afghanistan. If it means disconnecting from the world to get better that's what I will do. I have to go inside, in there I can hurt myself, protect others and maybe, just maybe, I can fix myself. The problem with doing this, I had a fiancée. The writing was on the wall for us and it wasn't long before she was moving out. This was nothing to do with my illness, I am hell to live with. I am too particular about every thing. Although I am upset, I am relieved, now I can really shut myself away, I no longer have to put anyone else first. It was now about me; fighting Afghanistan, fighting to keep my career and fighting to keep my sanity.

Another appointment was made with my psychiatrist, it was the same stuff coming from his mouth. I watch his lips move as he sits behind his desk. I noticed in our earlier appointments, he used to sit in the chair opposite me, now he has the safety of his desk to hide behind. The appointment was all about anti-depressants. I refuse to have them, I am not depressed, I don't need them, I just need a chance of a well-structured, thought-out programme. I need a second opinion, I need answers, why the hell wasn't I getting better? I type a letter to the psychiatrist, stating my feelings about anti-depressant medication and the breakdown of our relationship. I formally request a second opinion, I no longer wish his input on my treatment. It takes months but with my doctors help I finally get my second opinion granted.

Another December comes and I have shut off totally, no more work, my home is where I am safe or alone on my bike or in the gym. The pain reminds me of who I once was. The second opinion is military, I find it hard, but I want answers, was I depressed or had my treatment just been a mess?

I have to drive for hours, I have several different routes planned, in case I need to divert for any reason. I finally arrive at an army unit with a DCMH attached to it, I know the second opinion is to be from another military psychiatrist. I have to have answers, I will tell him everything, there are no reasons to hold back. I am cornered and fighting for what is most important to me, my career.

The place seems lighter than the one I have been visiting, I don't have any nerves. Strange really, should I be nervous? I remember some of my past fights, where my nerves used to steady me before I got into the ring. I don't have long to wait, a gent is holding out his hand, no uniform, he introduces himself to me; he is the psychiatrist I am here to see. He asks if I want a coffee and I do, I had been on the road for hours and 160 miles. The coffee is fresh, he has my notes, there is no point holding back, I start to talk about everything, the hours roll by.

It is now his turn to talk as I had bombarded him with so much information. He sat and took it, obviously this guy had done some homework about me and I would guarantee he would have had a phone call from my previous shrink. I sit uncomfortably but maintaining good eye contact, waiting for his opinion on my condition. Would they hold ranks and say the same things?

He is surprised I hadn't been connected with the psychologist and had formal Cognitive Behavioural Therapy (CBT). He thought my exposure programme was flawed, maybe because I had a hand in designing it. He said I was experiencing things at level ten and then back to one or two then nine or ten and that my brain couldn't cope with going from an easy level of exposure to situations which I associated with Afghanistan, to extreme ones. It needed to start from level one then on to ten.  Did I just hear correct?

He wasn't going to push me on to anti-depressants either; in his opinion at this time I didn't need them and pushing someone down a route they don't want to go is always counter productive. I stopped listening, I wanted to continue, this guy in front of me was giving me the answers I had desperately been seeking and he was answering some of my whys. He just said no anti-depressant tablets, not depressed, I need a structure and he wants me to have some sessions of CBT with the psychologist.

I had been giving myself hell for months thinking it was my fault, now I felt it wasn't just me. Others need to take responsibility for things not moving forward as quickly as they could have. With a little structure, I would be back, maybe I will be able to sleep through the night, maybe I can stop seeing and thinking about Afghanistan. The appointment came to a close and as I stood I felt weak but also that a big weight had been lifted from me. We made a further appointment in a month's time. He left me with one question he wanted me to ask myself over the next few weeks. If I returned to flying would I be able to fly in an operational environment again?

# Chapter Twenty nine

# Complete Bike Therapy

This question haunted me, both day and night. Christmas had arrived again, I didn't know where time is going, every day was the same, the same routine. I started to feel ill but thought I could train through it. Now I had some answers, my body needed some time to shut off and work out what was going on. It needed me to stop feeling the pain in the gym and really think about what had been said, could I fly again?

I had no choice but to stay in bed and contemplate the question. The illness wiped me out for most of Christmas and New Year. Now I know I am ill as I can't even muster any energy to go to the gym. This is the first time I had taken two weeks off since I started training 20 years ago.

I have to find some new energy to go to my second appointment with my new psychiatrist. I have a truthful answer to his question about flying operationally again. I sit waiting for him, today he is wearing uniform, not that it matters. We sit in his office which he has set out so he can't hide behind a desk. You always have his full attention. I sit looking at him; it is pointless hiding it. After the pleasantries and a chat about how ill I have been, I give him an answer to his question. No longer could I honestly put on a helicopter helmet get on board as a crew member and guarantee I wouldn't have any intrusive thoughts about Afghanistan.

It has beaten me, they have all won, my life is over, I have failed. He takes a time to think about it and he thanks me for being totally honest Now he wants to try to straighten me out enough so I can have some sort of normal life back. He places me on long term sick leave, no more gardening leave from the squadron. He is going to recommend for medical discharge from the armed forces, unfit for service due to PTSD. I sit there numb, my heart sinks, my head in overdrive with a mixture of thoughts and images.

Afghanistan, PTSD ... I thought I only had PTSR. How had I developed the full blown disorder? I had let myself down, I had no fight left in me, something else was happening. I could feel an old set of feelings and thoughts joining me from my past, I knew what they were because I had no strength left. The darkness was returning.

The psychiatrist is still talking, I pick up on some words but I need to put my attention elsewhere. I need to stop the darkness from returning. He was recommending a CBT programme and a structured mini-desensitisation programme, so I could try and live a normal life again. He said this will probably stay with me for a while, if not forever, I will get some normality back but not everything and some traumatic jobs I will never be able to do. Another question flashes into my head, what employer will ever want to employ me? My life has been the military what do I have to offer the world? I am broken, who will ever want me? I want to blame someone else; the only person I can blame is myself.

The official CBT starts when I return to my CPN at the DCMH further south. I want to keep a low profile and avoid the psychiatrist there, things don't feel right here now. I meet the psychologist who will be running me through CBT, with her is my CPN. I am glad she is here she understands me, but she has some news, I can see it in her face I am not going to like it. She knows me well enough to straight talk, she is being deployed to Afghanistan and I will be assigned to another new CPN. My head races I have to start again, not just with one person but with two, a CPN and a psychologist. Every time I step forward, something hits me and sends me backwards. The only constant I get is pain, she already knows this, but I want the psychologist to understand how hard I push in the gym and on long rides and that this keeps me in check, this keeps my balance.

The psychologist thinks I need a new focus and some way of not hurting myself. I smile, there is something troubling me about her and I cannot put my finger on it. She draws a few diagrams, I nod and smile, then it comes to me why she is troubling me. She is treating me like an idiot, I have intelligence, I have seen her sort before in my past. I want her to help me and this is meant to be a two way street, I seem to be going down a one way system alone.

My CPN was departing very soon, I was going to be alone at DCMH. I have been introduced to my new one, she doesn't have the same understanding, she was like the psychologist. I will tell them everything, I have to if I want to be normal again. I decide I want to speak to my doctor at Odiham, I need to see an old friend. It takes a while for me to get there as I hate going anywhere near Odiham, too many memories. I don't need any more reminders of my past.

I don't sit in reception, I go in the back door to the medical centre. The doctor knows I have to avoid people; it is hard enough getting there without seeing somebody who may push my buttons. It is great to see her, she has some news for me, she is leaving the military and moving on. She has had had enough, she has a new life, a recent marriage and new family in the next six months. I am happy, so happy for her, she is too good for the military system, she cares too much. I don't know why I feel my eyes welling up with tears, one escapes and rolls down my cheek. I apologise to her and explain it happens a lot lately. When I hear happy and sad news, my tears are replaced with rage in myself for showing weakness, I am a seesaw of emotions.

My head drifts off, I think the doctor knows how much I appreciate her and what she has done for me. I have friends both old and new, they all help in their own ways and they support me through different stages of this illness. I am now alone medically, without my doctor fighting for me, I was losing a friend and I was upset about it. I was only left with two allies at Odiham, my boss and an old friend, one guy who always visits me at home. He never has judged, he has watched and listened in disbelief as the system and colleagues have let me down.

Is it weakness or is it darkness? My head can no longer distinguish between the two. I am starting to do more extreme things, going out night riding in the early hours when I couldn't sleep because of the nightmares. I find country lanes, I have terrible lights on my bike and more than once I end in a ditch or in a hedge, the pain of a crash makes me smile. I always put my body before hurting my bike and I even have learnt to crash without damaging my bike. I am sick of not sleeping, I am waiting for this medical board; my life is ruined. After days of not sleeping I hit the bottle again. I know it isn't answer but it takes the edge off and helps on a night. I can get a few hours sleep before the booze wears off.

I need out, I have to escape so I buy a trailer to clip to my mountain bike to carry a Gore-Tex bivvy bag from my survival days. I pack it with four days of provisions, an AA Road Atlas and I buy a train ticket for Lands End. All people will see is a cyclist. No one has to know about my past. The shrink and CPN are concerned I don't turn the trip into a big training session. Like I will do that! What I had in mind was some CBT of my own - Complete Bike Therapy.

So I turned the key in my flat and got on my bike to the railway station. I felt good. People told me it doesn't matter if I make it or not, but to me it does. My head is destroyed but I have to see if I have still got what it takes; to push to the edge, to push my boundaries; to push my limits. I need to find myself.

I leave Lands End on my bike with no plan. I can survive I have the skills from the courses. I know which direction I want to go as there is only one way out of there. I have key waypoints in my head and the friends I want to see on the way to John O'Groats. It means going the long way but I have the time.

I spend some nights in ditches and hedge rows. Half way up the country, I buy a tent as my bivvy bag reminds me of work. I pitch my tent in woods because I want and need to be alone. I just cycle, pushing the mileage out. When everything aches, I switch off and do some extra miles; this is my test. The nights are still long, no matter which part of the country I am in, my nightmares follow me. I always find reminders of what I had become, Afghanistan never leaves me.

At the very least, my trip has given me back some enthusiasm; some fight to beat this. Afghanistan and the military haven't totally destroyed me. I have completed 1119 miles towing a trailer in a few weeks. I have my mental edge back and I know I can now control the darkness again.

I go back armed with new enthusiasm and the energy to embrace the official treatment plan from the CPN and psychologist. I want to get on aircraft again. I want to be normal and beat this. My medical board keeps getting cancelled though. Why do they keep building me up and then letting me down?

I want direction because at the moment I am lost. The bike mileage has caused an injury to my hips and I have to limit my long rides. No more long days of escaping for me, the rides were now harder with the pain so severe it makes me get off my bike and puke.

The hip pain has got worse and keeps me awake so the nightmares get worse. I discuss it with my psychiatrist and finally I agree to start on some anti-depressant medication to take the edge off and maybe stabilise me at night. I hate tablets but he makes a good argument for taking them. No longer does it matter if I am on them or not, I am never flying again.

After just a few weeks my mattress is destroyed with sweat. I have to stop taking the tablets, no longer can I wake up from my nightmares, the tablets won't let me; but tablets are no answer to this problem.

# Chapter Thirty

# An Honourable Discharge

The flood gates have truly opened, I am again engulfed in darkness, the darkness which I promised myself I would never return to. It now clouds my every thought both night and day. I need pain, I no longer care if I live or die. Death is favourable, my life is miserable, what is the point in it anymore?

The structured desensitisation programme is taking place at Brize Norton, it is pushing me further backwards. I sit on one of the Tristars and my head just spins. I want to be sick, I cannot stand this, my psychologist and CPN are with me. They explain I need to sit through the waves of emotion. I look forward, the aircraft appears to be rocking. My eyes are playing tricks on me, sweat drips off my hands, the tunnel of darkness encloses in.

I hate being anywhere near planes, they are reminding me that I was aircrew. They remind me of Afghanistan and how I have failed and that I am weak and broken. Why do they want to keep reminding me in this way?

Sleep is now worse than ever, I have up to four days of being awake, too scared to close my eyes. I am tired, tired of my nightmares, sleep now has to be booze induced.

A crunch day arrives when I attend my medical board and I so want some closure. I have had the procedure explained to me. Two doctors will see me and the second one will be the president of the board and will decided my future. I am alone, I had arranged a chaperone who would attend with me but they changed the dates at the last minute and I ended up alone. They seem to be conspiring against me, why do they the keep changing things?

I set off early for the appointment. It was a long drive which I spend wondering what they are going to do to me. I walk into the building, my heart is pounding, I have to keep alert. Today I cannot afford to get lost in my head. I have to be on top of things otherwise they will wreck me even further.

The waiting room, is neutral; almost too sterilised; someone enters in uniform. I assess him, he is wearing the same flying brevet (a badge signifying what trade I specialise in) that I once was so proud to wear. Another Loadmaster, what are the odds?

We nod and smile, he introduces himself as he pulls a file with my name on it out of his case. He is my promotion officer, he has been told to attend just in case there was a slim chance I can be moved to a different job. I am called to see the first doctor, he is an occupational specialist. I sit down and I recognise his face from somewhere in my past. He instantly pushes my buttons, I feel the rage inside me, he keeps belittling me and my job as a crewman. Who the hell did this guy think he is?

He didn't have a clue what crewman did, what is his problem? Is this a personnel vendetta against crewman or was it all aircrew? I shake as the rage pumps through my veins, this meeting is over. He recommends I am unfit for any military job, he stands and stretches out his hand. I look at it and then I look into his eyes, I turn and walk, slamming the door behind me.

Rage is flowing through me, I have to run, I have to get

out before I do something which I will regret. My promotion officer charges after me seeing something is wrong. He tries to calm me, I shake, rage pours out, tears roll down my cheeks. I battle to stay in control, he talks some sense back into me. I have to sit with the president of the medical board next; I needed to get a balance back. He knows my career is over but he manages to make me hate myself even more when he tells me I would have been promoted this year. I would have made it. I am stunned. He is trying to make me realise what I had achieved and that I always bounced back every time of asking and that the service had recognised this ability in me.

I feel sick, I didn't think I could feel any worse, the rage had turned to hate. I hated myself, I nearly had made it and I had failed. It was then time to meet the president of the board; can he make me feel any worse than I already did?

I sit in front of him, we started to chat, instantly he was more sensitive to my condition. He voiced his concerns; why didn't I receive debriefs on returning from operations or after the missile? Why had the squadron left me at home? Why had my treatment been so disjointed?

I talked through all of his questions, I will never blame anyone except myself, I wanted some good to come from all of this. All I wanted was for him to make sure it wouldn't happen to other people returning in the future. Afghanistan was here to stay and people are having a hard time normalising it. He ended our discussion with me feeling I had taken too much of his time already. He was to recommend I was unfit for service. I will be medically discharged for PTSD because of the aircraft incident in Afghanistan. The whole process will take six months to process. That is it, I am finished.

The decision has given me no comfort; it has driven me deeper into darkness. A social worker from the Soldiers Sailors Airman and Families Association (SSAFA) has started to visit me from Odiham. Usually she gives me warning she is coming to see me, but one day she calls in on the off chance. This was lucky as I was having one of my darker days. She is shocked at how everything has finally taken its toll, my medical board, the desensitisation programme and my hip injury. She could see I was spinning out of control.

She left to make phone calls and a few days later she phones me and passes an idea by me. She wants me to leave my flat as it is too near Odiham and the Chinooks. She can arrange a house near Brize Norton where I can be properly monitored by the medical services based there and I don't have to travel so much for the desensitisation programme. Her words just bounce off me. I just don't care what they do to me anymore.

In order to get back in control, I have entered another bike event, despite the pain of my hips. It's a race and I end up hitting a tree in a freak accident, damaging my wrist. I smiled as the pain enters my body, my bike is fine so I can continue. I remount and think about the pro cyclists who ride with broken bones, my wrist is swelling. I find it hard to grip the handle bars but I push on as it is only a short one today. I only have another 45 miles to go and I ride into second place all the way with my wrist and hips absolutely screaming in pain.

Now I am totally broken, my head, my wrist and hips. I cannot train any longer, what can I do for pain? I remember having tattoos and I have wanted a new one. Every picture on my body symbolises some significant event of my past. I need a new one to signify this event. An idea pops into my head, I switch on the Internet and start searching for images. I find one but it is not quite right, it will need some custom work. I find a tattooist's website who is obviously pro-forces and supportive of troops. I look at his work, he is for me, I book an appointment. We discuss my design idea, he will customise one of the images for me and it will take four hours split into two sessions. I smile at the thought of it, it will help focus my head away from the darkness for a time.

After some more sleepless nights, in the end I succumb to the bottle for the few precious hours' sleep it gives me. The answer comes to me in a booze hazed day. I no longer can continue, I need to be shot. I need an honourable death, I have nothing left. If I can get hold of a 9mm it will be over, an overdose isn't the way out, I need to die with honour. One shot, one kill, it is the only way.

Every flashback to Afghanistan made the need to end it grow stronger; I need a pistol to take my head off. I drive my car in a reckless manner, wanting to crash or be taken out by another vehicle. The central reservations on motorways invite me. I think of reasons not to, they are getting harder to find. The only one which keeps me going is other people, as I cannot destroy anyone else's life only my own. I no longer have anything, my job, my training, my girlfriend. I had lost the lot, the darkness had won.

The removal vans have arrived to take me to Brize Norton. I wonder if this is a fresh start or the final nail in my coffin. I don't care either way, I am moving from Chinooks flying over me daily.

I have no friends here, I was never stationed here at Brize Norton, I am alone. I now come under the care of two people from the admin and welfare section, I am sure they are glad to have a nut job to look after. When I meet them, I instantly I warm to them. I am made to feel a part of the military again. They show me around and offer to help in any way they can. I may be getting discharged but they want me to leave with a different perspective of my time with the military, they want to show me a compassionate side. They clearly care and I wouldn't be alone again.

The new environment is making the days long but the nights longer. The constant plane noise makes the darkness come. I cannot hit the gym, I need help. I decided I better ask for it, I speak with my psychologist, she decides on another new anti-depressant tablet. I am filled with fear with what this may do to me after last time. I start to take them but within days a rage inside surfaces, a rage so vile I cannot control it.

I lock the door and hide the key, I need to protect the world from me. I look outside my kitchen window, a woman pushing a pram, the rage inside me spills over. I want either her dead or me, it doesn't matter which. I see my hands close around the handle of a carving knife, pulling it out of the block. "No!," my voice of reason, I release my grip, the knife falls to the floor, the woman continues walking. I fall to my knees, shaking punching the floor, I need pain. My knuckles soon swell. I read the tablet side effects, suicidal thoughts are one of them. I already have them but now they could spill over onto some innocent people. I have to stop taking them. Back to square one, no sleep.

Day four and I haven't closed my eyes. I am tired, angry and I need to sleep. I push my fingers in my ears to drown out the plane noise. Sod it I need a beer. I head into the local town and start on a session. I need to collapse. I drink and drink, not caring what may happen as long as I can sleep. I stumble from bar to bar and end up in the wrong one. Music is playing, the bass is too loud and a pressure wave of music hits my body. Everything blurs, the Apache, the missile, Helmand.

I blink and feel another pressure wave, I am trapped inside the flashbacks. I put my drink down. Tonight I have to die. I have a replica weapon at home. I reckon if I pull the gun on the guard force at the unit, they will shoot me. It will be a fantastic honourable death.

I jump in a taxi with a plan forming to end it all. Back at the base, my plan is formed but something keeps delaying me. Something inside is telling me I have other options and I am to try them first. I pick up the phone and dial all the help lines on the base. I call the padre, the shrinks, the medics but nobody answers. That is the confirmation I need; it is my time.

Wait, I have one more number, someone told me I wouldn't be alone. I call her my new RAF contact the boss of the admin section. It is the early hours, will she answer?

I hear her voice, dazed and tired. I am babbling, my thoughts come out in random sentences all of them with the same meaning. I have nothing left I need to end it all. She panics and calls the military police, they arrive blue lights blazing. Now I have a situation to deal with. Some idiot copper outside calling me mate, telling me to stop being stupid. This guy is making me worse, the rage hits harder and harder. I am trapped if I head out of the house I will not get my chance to be shot and I need to be shot.

I phone a few people I need to say goodbye to but I know I am just playing for time. I want them to know what has happened I may not be missing an arm or a leg, but I am missing something. The copper taps again. This guy is pissing me off, they have no jurisdiction here, they cannot break in. I am on civilian ground and the door is solid. Fuck 'em, they can watch my death.

I hear a new voice when a new set of police uniforms appear - it's the Thames Valley Armed Police. I smile as at last someone wants me to die; this is my chance to be shot. I need a new plan, come on think tactics.

The front door, there are two of them, threaten them, if they come through, knife the first, the second will have to shoot me. I get my knives out, the time is now. I decide I have to die in uniform, I go upstairs, put it on, the thing I was once was most proud to wear; now in my death it will be remembered.

More blue lights outside, this time paramedics as they must have realised this is about to get bloody. They are only needed to mop up. Then from the darkness another figure arrives. Not only did she answer her phone, she has driven up to talk to me, to try and sort this out. I owe her that at least as I pulled her into this

I need to explain why so we chat through the window with the police just behind her. My knives are ready in case they think they can use her as a distraction. They didn't know how my brain worked, I had already planned and re-planned their every move. A friend comes on the phone I pass it through the window, I can hear him scream for them to stand down. He knows what I want.

All I really long for is sleep, a sleep so strong, I cannot wake, no more nightmares, there is only one way to have that happen. I start to see sense, she is calming me down, reassuring me that together we can sort this out, that I am no longer alone. I see it in her eyes, it isn't hollow words, I need to give her a chance, I have to.

The police stand back, they now understand I wanted them to shoot. She has told them I have PTSD, they realise I am injured. Soon things are back on a level, I agree to let them in. We compromise, I hand over my weapons and they will treat me with respect, no cuffs, no manhandling.

I turn the key, the armed officers enter, no pistols just a Taser. That wont kill me and they are true to our agreement. I get a quick pat down and a check for other weapons before allowing the others in. I have to agree to go to a mental hospital and be admitted. I will go on a voluntary basis, if not I will be sectioned and I will lose total control.

# CHAPTER THIRTY-ONE

# TALKING TO MY MIND

The mental ward in Oxford isn't much to talk about; people are here with all sorts of different problems. I just want to be alone. The ward is semi-secure, doors and windows are locked and patrols are in operation.

I start to switch back on. I note patrol timings, areas where I can escape. Soon have got the plan formed, I am not on medication so have full control of my body and mind. The patrols are every 15 minutes, that is vast amount of time. First they will search the ward, every bathroom and room before calling the police. I don't know their response time but I am here voluntarily so I won't be high priority. It didn't matter as they will never find me. The distance I will have covered will be massive.

I sit on the window ledge of my room, observing the staff, the patients, mentally assessing each one of them. I don't want to mix with them, everyone here has had their problems they all have a story. None of them are military, I can tell by their actions and their voices. They are not tuned in like I am. These people will not understand what has driven me here.

I find an easy way of escape, my window has some big security flaw in it. I can pop it in seconds, the only problem in going through it is they will know I have gone and instantly search outside. I can set up a diversion though, I keep tweaking my plan of escape, but why do I need to escape? I feel safe here, I am locked away, I cannot hurt anyone they are protected from me and someone is keeping an eye on me.

Doctors never get to you quickly it has been 36 hours and I still haven't been seen by anyone qualified. Only a couple of house doctors but no one who may be able to give me a few answers. I finally sit down with the civilian psychiatrist, she has two male nurses with her, am I that much of a threat?

I tell her everything, she may have an answer, she keeps checking her watch; clearly she has more important things to do. Finally she asks, "Will I hurt myself or anyone else in my present state of mind?"

I tell her that it's obvious I am quite clearly in control and that the drugs last night gave me a little respite. I am good for a few days now, she goes on to tell me they are not equipped for my kind of trauma. I stop listening, pass the buck, I am military you are NHS; you don't care what happens, patch me up and send me on my way. Thanks for nothing.

My escape plan was academic in the end as the welfare officer picked me up from the ward and returned me to the house. Things don't feel right I need to be out of here. I don't know where I will go, anywhere but here. I am on sick leave but I am still in the military so I cannot leave yet. I have to attend the doctors and the psychologist yet again. The doctor is fine, very understanding and she tries to focus my attention onto getting myself sorted for civilian life. I have six months before my official discharge. She asks what I am planning to do.

The thought of being back in a work environment, especially a new civilian one gives me shudders. I hate being around people, I need to be alone. At least being alone I can control what is going on in my head. I cannot make plans for my future because I don't have one. Sit blank, let her do her job, she has experience of PTSD. Let her talk, then I can just leave.

Then it's time for the psychologist, she just doesn't understand me. Her opening line of running a booze factory has touched a big nerve; I switch off from her and go through the motions. My insides are screaming, if you didn't sleep for four days and had constant intrusive thoughts and flashbacks, what the hell would you do to finally switch off your brain?

I feel weak and vulnerable, I take a gulp of air and find myself asking her for help, for a different type of anti-depressant, I just want her to do one thing for me, lock me away until the side effects have worn off so I don't hurt myself or anyone else. She can't do that for me, I can have the tablets but I have to go it alone, in the house.

I cannot fight this alone in my weakened state, the darkness was back it had been let loose within my head. Just give me some mind altering drugs and I feared what may happen. The appointment was going nowhere, we had hit a brick wall, a stalemate. I was asking for help, she couldn't give it to me. All she saw was the booze clouding me, not the reasons behind the booze. Yet another doctor patient relationship was broken, any trust or rapport had gone. I had to get out and try and sort this myself, they won't help me, they had had over two years and I have got to the edge and I keep losing my balance and falling backwards. I need a rope and someone to help pull me up or show me how to climb again. Or one to hang myself with.

I have to leave so I decide on a road trip North to visit close friends. I need to try and get some normality back. Being around close friends helps, I can detach myself from my life and focus on something else. They all know what is happening, they have seen me get worse over the last two years and they want to help. I decide to visit friends who know about the military. They have left now but, having spent years in it, they understand my language and the system. I am hoping they can help guide me through the leaving process. The challenges of leaving are tough but leaving with a problem, when it isn't your choice to leave, is even tougher.

I make two stops in Northumberland. At the second, we spend a night chatting things over. He is a friend from my early Chinook days, he has left the military and understands me. He was the one who screamed at the police down the phone to stand down a few weeks ago. He made no bones about it, he knows I am on the ragged edge and I will be dead soon if we don't find some hope, some way of beating this. As we chat, I keep coming back to the name of a charity. It was brought to my attention months before by a neighbour when she too was concerned for my safety and welfare.

When I approached the subject of outside help with the military specialist, they had selective hearing or they would tell me it could counter the treatment plan they had in place for me and that I wasn't to engage with any alternative therapy. Their treatment hadn't done anything. I had got worse not better. It was time for me to take control and make my own plan, I will make a call to this charity.

Saturday afternoon and my fingers shake as I punch in the numbers to call the charity 'Talking2Minds'. They have a website and it reads well. It appears to be run by guys like me, ex-forces, who have gone through hell and have found a way to get rid of their PTSD. I may have a chance, a way of getting rid of this thing, maybe the experts are wrong and I can be fixed and this won't be with me for ever. A male voice picks up the phone, my stomach is a washing machine on its spin cycle.

We chat freely, instantly we have the same language not only from the military but from PTSD. He starts to finish my sentences, sentences which no one else has comprehended. He really did understand this thing, this guy knew how it felt, he knew how dark I had become. We continued to chat, again my flood gates opened. Then he promised that I would never be alone again, the charity would help me and if the military didn't like it, they wouldn't have to know. I can see the first signs of a real hope for the first time in years.

This guy is convinced the Talking2Minds process will change me and get rid of my PTSD. All I have to do is to send him an e-mail and he would get me on a course as quickly as he could because he was concerned for my safety. He knew I had gone over the edge. I put the phone down, unable to control the tears. When I finally realised what had happened I just smiled as I might have a future.

I started to chat with my friend, I started to run with future plans, maybe rent his house, go to college, move away, be myself again, everything was flooding in. The darkness is being pushed to one side.

We both sit there, happy this charity has given me hope; we decide it is time to celebrate with a few beers in town. I feel I am again on top of things, I don't need to hide away from the world, a few beers won't hurt because today I can see an end in sight. The place starts to get busy, I need to keep my head, I am starting to get unnerved again, people, noise. I close my eyes, think of the hope I have. Come on, I can do this, it will pass. I hit the bottle that little bit more, my nerves increase as more people arrive. We leave to another bar. I have to keep control. I am stronger than this, more crowds and more noise, it hits me like a sledge hammer. What I had pushed to one side earlier today, has now returned with a greater vengeance. It is teaching me a lesson in what happens when or if I dare to see a future without it.

I start to panic, I don't want to hurt anyone or myself. I won't let it beat me. A new song comes on with a heavy bass and a pressure wave to match. No, no, no, I am not going back there. I smell it, the hydraulic oil, I close my eyes. I am not there. I am not there. I open them and I am there. The Apache, the missile, I tense as here it comes again.

I need to run, I need out, I turn, where is my friend? I start to shake, keep control.

Whack! Another pressure wave hits me. My mind is lost in the past, more panic.

Everyone's eyes are burning into me, why are they all watching me? I have to run, I have to die. I head out into the quiet darkness of the street. I need to find a church; I need to find a peaceful place to make a plan. There is no way of getting shot. I will go to the beach and do a Reggie Perrin.

I know it is miles away but a taxi will take me in minutes. I don't need money where I am going. I will walk into the surf, no one will ever find me. I'll be gone, I will leave my wallet so people know not to look for me, they will understand. I find what looks like a church. A security guard's outside. Shit this isn't a church, it's a hospital! He starts to ask questions, questions only a member of the forces can ask. His language is forces talk, how does he know?

He realises I need help, he asks me in for a brew, so I follow him and he introduces me to the charge nurse. With a brew in front of me, I don't know how it came out, but it did and they both stand back. They could hear I was serious about suicide. I had had enough I was tired, they try to turn me back in time.

I start to babble about a charity that promised me to

help. The nurse dials the number but gets an answer phone. Why didn't they answer? I try again, he will hear it this time and answer? The answer phone again, I start to get agitated. I need out, the security guard has locked the door. I am trapped. I start to weigh up my options, he hasn't got a weapon. I am younger fitter and I know how to fight.

I can see concern spreads across their faces almost as if they can see into my head. I need to be seen by a qualified trauma team, calls are made. I keep assessing a way out without hurting anyone. The security guard is opening the door and in come reinforcements. I am to be transferred to a different hospital and then my mental state will be assessed. I no longer care. They can do whatever they like and I know another time will come. I won't try to push my darkness away again, I have learnt my lesson.

I am strapped in the ambulance, a paramedic is in the back monitoring me. Why the straps? I chat with him, I will make him see the real me, soon he is telling me he spent some time in the Marines. He looks me in the eyes and tells me to pull myself together and get a grip. Rage hits and I want to smash him to pieces, these straps I can pop. I have use of my hands, I have to keep control, if not I will go to jail because I will smash him into pieces. I tell myself to blank out his face and voice. Why the hell didn't he understand me?

I sussed that I needed to know why so I re-engaged with our chat, hiding the rage inside. He soon answers my question and it's clear this idiot has never seen active service. It's no wonder he doesn't understand. The trauma team soon arrive and I am again assessed as unstable due to PTSD. I will be transferred to a mental ward in South Shields for my safety and the safety of others.

A different ambulance crew transport me, I watch out of the window. I know South Shields as it is where I finished the Great North Run. I smile because I know which way to go if I decide I have to run. On the way in, I am looking at everything, electronic door locks, reception windows, which way I need to turn, which way staff will be coming at me. This place is more secure than Oxford but, give it time, I'll find a way out. I will have a plan of escape.

I am to be housed in a twin room with someone. This is another kind of hell as I hate new people. If he pushes me I will snap, even at friend's houses I have to lock a door or move furniture so I'm locked in on my own. I tell this to the nurse who is assigned to me; she decides it is safer for everyone if I have my own room.

She stays with me all day, I realise I am on suicide watch. I don't mind. She is friendly and has a compassion I haven't seen in many. We chat and soon bond and in a way she reminds me of one of my CPNs, the one who really understood me and the one who had to leave for Afghanistan. This nurse had experienced something in her life which gave her some understanding about some of the things inside me.

So I regain control; my darkness is giving me a chance because it knows it can remind me when it needs to. I talk about the charity I had phoned and she wants to take a look at them for me. As we talk, she keeps telling me I will be safe and then a door slams. I look to the left, not again, my heart races I know where I am my darkness keeping me on the edge.

When I come back from it, she is still here, she asked me if I'm OK. She asks if I had just been back there, back to Afghanistan. My eyes fill with tears as I nod at her. I decide to tell her all about Afghanistan, not just the missile flashbacks but everything including the things you don't see on the news and I've not put in this book to spare the reader. She is shocked at what I now perceive as normality.

My phone then rings. I look down, it was Talking2Minds calling. I have to answer, we chat for the second time in 24 hours. I tell him about my meltdown, he understands, no judgement, just concern because he knows how I feel, with this my hope returns.

He tells me, "Get yourself signed out of there by the end of the week. We are going to take you to a place in France next week and treat you. You will get your life back, you are never alone."

The reassurance and the confidence he has in the treatment sends me into floods of tears. My emotions are raw, the nurse looks on and squeezes my hand. I will be safe now. During the night I ask to be locked in. They hand me a sedative to sleep. In strange places I have to keep fully clothed ready to run, ready to get out.

The drugs wear off, I am still fully clothed. I can wander around the ward but I want to stay here, in the safety of my room. A new nurse taps on my door and tells me the professor of psychiatry is here to chat with me. He is in charge of the ward, we chat about treatments and what has happened.

I am getting used to these people, it is the same questions. I only need to respond to a couple and listen for their answers before I can tell if they will or won't help me, if they are genuine or just all talk.

This guy was genuine.

He then asks me something, something no one has asked me, "What did I want them to do?"

The answer was a simple one, just keep me locked away and safe. The professor is a breath of fresh air, he doesn't pretend to understand war trauma, but he has an open mind. His ward has a range of treatments from the standard to the more relaxing and alternative Indian head massage. A gym has been built on the side for patients to workout and he somehow understands how people become trapped.

I speak again of Talking2Minds and I ask him to look into them. They had given me hope but inside I still had doubts. The meeting came to close when he handed me the NHS NICE guidelines for PTSD. He had listened to everything. I didn't even notice the nurse leaving to get a copy of the booklet.

"Inside you may find some answers to your questions," he said with a smile.

Over the week I read it and understand what the military tried to do, but why had they kept this document away from me? The knowledge would have helped me. The more I read, the more understanding I got about the treatments like EMDR and CBT and how many sessions it would take to be successful. It told of how structures for desensitisation should be monitored closely. NICE described in detail all the recommended anti-depressant drugs and all of their side effects. I'd had them all and I found this all very enlightening.

The week passed quickly. My friend keeps visiting and it is good to see him. He brings DVDs for me to watch; all funny ones he'd screened for no loud bangs. We laugh and joke. He had a sense of humour as he tried getting One Flew over the Cuckoos Nest.

Talking2Minds keep checking in too. Every time we speak the hope inside of me grows that little bit bigger. My CPN from DCMH calls but no longer will I allow them in. I don't want them involved now, they have had their chance and I have got a lot worse. The conversations I have on the phone prove they didn't care, they just want me contained. I felt safe here on the ward, I had my moments, my emotions were still raw, but I was safe. My darkness couldn't hurt me here, it couldn't destroy the glimmer of hope I now had.

Days later the Professor comes back to me with an answer about Talking2Minds.

He said, "To be honest it's the best thing you can do. I don't understand their treatments or approach, but what I do know from years of working in mental health is a schizophrenic patients fixes a schizophrenic patient."

I smile in recognition and he continues, "We doctors and nurses are just guides we don't fix. People with like illnesses fix one another. Being able to engage and work with people who have served and understand the military and PTSD will be the best thing you can do."

My decision is made. I will go for treatment with Talking2Minds.

What did I have to lose?

# EPILOGUE

As I sit here in France, feeling the warm mountain air blow around me from the Pyrenees, I smile and I will try and put into words how I feel now.

The process worked, my nightmares stopped. I don't want to explain the process. If you decide it is right for you, please go and experience it without my spin on things. The process cannot remove memories, but what it does do, is remove the negative connections your mind places on the events of the past.

People and friends all want to know how, why and how do I know it won't happen again? Let me take a little more of your time and try to explain.

Now you have read this book, you know I have had these feelings for years. For years I could control them, but when my rucksack got so full of memories, I was stuck up my mountainside of life again and I was pulled backwards towards the darkness. I had to take off my rucksack and really sort out what I was carrying.

Every memory I was carrying seemed to get heavier with time. I think some of the memories were covered in mud. When I put them in my bag, the mud stuck and merged with all my past childhood memories to the point where everything congealed into a heavy load.

I couldn't see anything clearly anymore. The past, which I thought I had moved away from by running to the military, became muddy again. I was lucky because some memories were cleaned by my homeopath and I had a few years of peace.

Then the next muddy memory appeared and the mud started to stick again. When I sought help from different places, some tried to give me a sponge to clean the memories, but it was dry, the water was missing.

Now I have washed all my memories down, cleaned them, dried them and I have learnt why I was carrying them. Mud cannot ever stick to them again because they are now in a clear, sealed, vacuum bag, taking up less space in my rucksack, protected from any new mud life has to offer. I am happy to carry them in life and I can look at them through the clear plastic because every memory and experience has enabled me to learn and develop myself. Why would I want to leave them behind or forget them?

Talking2Minds gave me a new sponge and fresh water; they also showed me a way of keeping my sponge clean and a way of getting fresh clean water. I have a choice to keep a clean sponge or use a muddy one. I embraced my new skills, but I needed to know more. I needed to know how the sponge was formed and where the water came from, so I undertook some personal development courses and I still have lots to learn.

Do I ever think I will find the source of the water? No, but it's a great path to follow and learn from. In learning about it, it has also assisted me in being able to show others how to clean their memories with sponges and fresh water. Now I can pick up my rucksack because it is lighter and start climbing my mountain of life again.

I was worried about letting go of some of my past memories. Would I lose the edge, my ability to push myself? Not just in my sports but in my life. If I put down the pain I had used for years what would I replace it with?

I had to take some scary steps, I had a choice to take them, I am glad I did, my sports have improved. I can also listen to my body; I can hear what it tells me now my memories are not full of voices of the past. I see myself in the mirror and somehow I look lighter without the pain of the past, my eyes are not so sunken and I find myself smiling.

At the start smiling felt strange, I didn't have the pain of my past, I missed it. It had been there for so long, but every smile is one which has been long overdue in life, it is OK not to have pain and enjoy life.

As I ride through life on my horse, I ask myself was I brave, was I a knight who had to protect? My armour never got put back on after my homeopath helped me remove it, I experienced PTSD without it. Now it is time to give my horse a rest and place my armour in a trunk. Somewhere where I can look at it because when I see it, it will remind me of how it once protected me. I ride now, I need no protection, I need no title, I am happy being me. I am more aware of people and situations, not just people from my past but people in my present.

Some people have tried to keep me there with my old memories, all of them are unaware of it, maybe it is because they have a few bad memories of their own. I totally understand they either needed me to stay there because it made them feel safe or they thought they were doing the best for me; I know they had my best interests at heart. I have no challenges with anyone, everyone has a choice and it is their choice how they want to treat me now. I have had to make a few tough life choices already and in future more will appear. That is all a part of being alive.

My past is my past, it isn't the hardest or darkest story you may read about; I wouldn't change a thing from it, not from my childhood or military career. I had some great times and experiences, sadly I couldn't remember the good ones because for every one bad memory, it stopped me remembering 100 good ones.

For everyone who was involved in past life and events, this is how I perceived things. They may see the events in a different way and that is perfect for them. My only wish is they can learn as much from me and my choices, as I learnt from them and the events they were involved with.

I have stepped out of the ring, I am no longer in a fight, there is no need for a referee to give me a count, I have tasted the canvas, now I have stepped through the ropes and I can stop fighting because I have the skills, abilities and awareness to move away from the fights life may have to offer. If a punch gets thrown in my direction I know what to do about.

Thank you old friends and new, for the love, support and understanding you and your families have shown me. Without you, the ending would have been different. I know some of the times we shared were hard, but the hardest times gave us greater understanding and friendships.

Thank you readers for taking the time to read about me; if you know me you may understand me a little better. The readers I don't know, I hope this will help you understand someone who may be suffering from the traumas of their past. Maybe there's something buried inside you and you've now decided it's the right time to do something about it.

I hope in reading this you may also have the courage to look outside the box, there are other treatments out there, you will find the one which is right for you. Your treatment maybe inside the box, there are no right or wrong ways as long as you get what you need from them. My boxes took me on a journey of Synergy, Neuro Linguistic Programming, Spectrum™ Therapy, Hypnosis and Reiki and I continue to develop my skills and knowledge in all of these fields and more, I want to keep looking at new boxes, who knows what is inside them.

You may ask can it ever to me again?

No, because Daylight Doesn't Appear Dark.

# THE JOURNEY CONTINUES

My name is Mick Stott and my company is called Quantum Performance, I am the designer and main provider of therapies used by the charity called Talking2Minds.

Having spent long hours in meditations that resulted in the production of programmes designed to help those who suffer from PTSD, I arrived at the decision to bring veterans from the UK to a remote village in the Pyrenees. This is the home of skylarks, owls, birds of prey and a host of wildlife. It is not only a great holiday home for my family but it is the training venue for other healing programmes and performance courses.

It was the first time that I had met Matt and was told of his journey so far. I am always careful not to set or establish any pre-conceptions of anyone as these can be obstructive when working objectively. As with all of the guys who have been in the mental health system when they arrive they are nervous and trust is the key issue, laced with fear this requires careful handling as these guys are all very physically capable of getting upset and reacting violently, as a result of their experiences when negative emotions are high confusion reigns.

In the opening sessions I remember looking at his face, he looked like a lost boy who had all of the physical attributes of a man, which in itself was something of a contradiction. He was getting ready to run from the off even though you could hear in his language the parts of him that knew he should stay as he wanted to get well, like so many others who cannot find their way back from their own inner world of pain.

It became apparent very quickly that Matt was going to need very careful handling as he had already shown his passport to his chosen therapist twice and was in the business of running, because the enemy inside was bigger and stronger than he could manage. It became apparent that what we were doing with Matt wasn't working as he wasn't engaging or looking any different and by day two of the programme this is highly unusual. The behaviours he demonstrated were still those of someone who was running as opposed to fighting, which highlighted to me that we needed to flex and approach things differently.

None of the other therapists wanted to work with him as he scared them with his manner and appeared to be difficult in every way, he also behaved in a way that was unpredictable, which unnerved people. I decided to take up the challenge as ultimately he was my responsibility and we needed to get him to a better place quickly if he was going to leave us with a belief that he could change and get well.

In the first few sessions Matt was having problems turning off his thinking mind and didn't really get what we were doing so I used some interventions that are designed to break down beliefs quickly and remove the negative charge from memories that had brought him to this point. He was surprised to learn that the problems he had experienced on operations were not really the main contributing factor to his problem it was just the straw that broke the camels back.

We worked with Matt and our unique programme called Synergy worked its magic and he started to change and more importantly feel the changes himself. Matt was significant in the development of Spectrum Therapy™ as his conscious logical mind got in the way regularly, and it was the introduction of colours and sensations that got him to switch off, changing with each intervention and realising the possibilities that were becoming more and more apparent.

A period of months went by and Matt decided to train as a Practitioner and then on to a Master Practitioner, so that he could help others get what he got. It was when I saw him engage with a group of guys who arrived for the same programme one year later on from his own that made me realise what a truly changed person he was. After all according to the medical world once a PTSD sufferer always a sufferer, but Matt had a drive that would not allow anything to get in the way and he proved this by what he did.

Matt now works with Quantum Performance using the skills he learned in the Royal Air Force along with other skills that were dormant for the period he spent being unwell.

I wonder how many Matt's are out there who believe that others can but they cannot or that they are special cases in some way, well I can say from working with thousands of people that Matt proved to me that if you have a big enough reason to do something and someone shows you the way anything is possible.

You see its all about performance and the best man for the job and Matt is the best man for the job. He lost his way for a while but trusted in someone when he didn't want to and hoped that things would work out. He was prepared to put the effort in to change his story. He is now the star in his story and has defined himself in doing so as a courageous soul who is sensitive and caring to those he now helps move forward, for nothing other than the privilege of doing so.

This is a far cry from what was said about him when

he encountered his problems but it is not the critic who counts it is the man in the arena. These are not my words as they belong to someone more learned than I, they are, however, simple truths that hold true when you are looking for answers in life.

It was George Bernard Shaw who said the people who get the most from life are those who when they can't find the circumstances they want they create them. This is a great philosophy I add to this that to get the most from life you have to be prepared to trust be honest in all you do and give consent to receive help.

Matt assisted us all to learn more about the approach we use called Synergy he was also key to me writing and launching Spectrum Therapy™ because of the way he thought and responded to colour and sensations. He was proof that we could work with some of the most challenging people breaking some of the stereotypes associated with therapy.

Matt's journey will no doubt prove to be inspirational to those who feel they are beyond help and that change is impossible. His journey has only just begun and as it unfolds he will be at the forefront of an approach that is groundbreaking in all respects.

*Mick Stott*
Quantum Performance
www.quantumperformance.org

# talking 2 minds

UK Charity No. 1131142

Talking2Minds is the leading charity in the effective coaching and therapeutic treatment of PTSD amongst other stress related disorders. We specialise in helping those that are long term sufferers and those for which other therapies have not worked. We use a unique programme, Synergy, that utilizes a results focussed and extremely effective therapy called Spectrum Therapy™.

Many people are unaware of the true impact of Post Traumatic Stress Disorder until it becomes part of their lives.

If you've found your way to the end of Matt's book, there is a good chance that you, or someone you know, are one of the many hundreds of thousands of people in the UK affected by Post Traumatic Stress. You are not alone.

Talking2Minds is run by veterans in order to help veterans back to health as quickly as possible.

Talking2Minds therapy is for both serving and former forces, blue light services and civilian PTSD sufferers alike.

"The solution to any problem does not lie in the problem itself as it lies outside of the problem"

Talking2Minds specialises in treating the symptoms, effects and root cause of PTSD. Founded by Bob Paxman (former B Squadron 22 SAS) and his wife Kim, the Talking2Minds ethos is 'veterans helping veterans' and 'like helping like', meaning that there is a strong rapport and understanding at every level between the guest and the coach.

There is no need to revisit any traumatic memories with our process.

Talking2Minds is a Registered Charity.

The author grew up in Yorkshire, in quite a badly broken home, and suffered a very unhappy childhood that left him with unresolved issues which he carried with him to adulthood. Learning how to cope with life's problems through punishing himself with sport and exercise, the pain made him feel alive but he needed more, he needed too escape.

He joined the Royal Air Force at seventeen in his bid to escape from his past. Initially he served as a ground-based technician, retraining later as an "Air Loadmaster" aircrew on the Chinook helicopters.

Following a tour of duty in Iraq, combined with several stressful situations in his private life, he experienced a breakdown and attempted suicide. Coaxed back from the edge by a mixture of support, he was soon sent back into action again, this time serving in the Helmand, Afghanistan.

On his return home, he suffered another breakdown which eventually cost him his seventeen-year career within the RAF. He was diagnosed and subsequently medically discharged from service suffering with Post Traumatic Stress Disorder (PTSD).

During some of his lowest points in-between stays at two mental institutions for once again thinking the only option he had left from his nightmares was suicide, a charity called Talking2Minds was brought to his attention. The treatment he received stopped his nightmares and PTSD, his life was returned and he was finally able to start rebuilding.

Now a qualified Master Practitioner in Neuro Linguistic Programming (NLP), Hypnosis, Spectrum Therapy, Time Line Therapy and Reiki he has new skills to help himself and others.

www.eventhedaylight.com

Lightning Source UK Ltd.
Milton Keynes UK
03 March 2011

168569UK00001B/3/P